KEWPIE®

for Collectors

by John Axe

Published by 

Hobby House Press, Inc.
Grantsville, Maryland
www.hobbyhouse.com

Dedication

To my Kewpie® friends who helped me with the Kewpie® book in 1985 and who are no longer with us: Shirley Buchholz, Ralph Griffith, Lillian Mosley, Mona Nevins, Grayce Piemontesi, Lillian Rohaly, and Helen Sieverling.

Acknowledgments

I appreciate the help and advice, the sharing of collections, and the professional input from all the following without whom I could not have completed this project.

For permitting me to photograph valuable collections: Bette Ann Axe, Donna Felger, Shirley Karaba, Rosemary Hanline, Wanda Lodwick, Mona Nevins, and Karen Shaker.

For assistance and cooperation, the Reference/Special Collections Librarians were wonderful at the Akron/Summit County Public Library, Cleveland Public Library and the Public Library of Youngstown and Mahoning County.

Companies and organizations and individuals within them who were indispensable: Joe Bartolotta and Margiann Flanagan of Cameo Collectibles; Susan Bickert of The German Doll Company; Susan Judge and Florence Theriault of Theriault's; Audrey Looman, President of the International Rose O'Neill Society; Donna Mehalco, Branch Manager, and Theresa Thompson, Operations Assistant at ComDoc; Susan Scott, President of the Bonniebrook Historical Society; Nancy Villaseñor-Cordaro, former president of Jesco Imports, Inc.; Tom Skahill, Consultant of Jesco Imports, Inc.; and most of all, James E. Skahill, CEO of Jesco Imports, Inc.

For turning all this into a finished book, the staff of Hobby House Press, especially Gary R. Ruddell, Brenda Wiseman, Theresa Black, and Sherry White.

The metric conversions in this book have been rounded to the next whole number. To find an exact equivalent, multiply the number of inches by 2.54cm.

Additional copies of this book may be purchased at $27.95 (plus postage and handling) from
Hobby House Press, Inc.
1 Corporate Drive, Grantsville, MD 21536
1-800-554-1447
www.hobbyhouse.com
or from your favorite bookstore or dealer.

Printed in the United States of America

ISBN: 0-87588-666-3

Table of Contents

Foreword

Kewpie® is the first doll I ever knew by name. My sister Bette Ann got a *Kewpie* for Christmas when we were quite young. Everyone loved this doll because of the jolly look on its face and the cute presentation with *Kewpie* wearing a sunsuit. This was the fully-jointed composition version by Noma Electric (Effanbee) under license from Joseph L. Kallus in the late 1940s.

For many years we did not know the maker of the doll or that several years earlier someone named Rose O'Neill had invented *Kewpie*. As an adult, I became a serious doll collector, although I had collected dolls most of my life. Collectors want to know as many facts and details as possible about the things that they prize. In 1985, my findings about *Kewpie* were compiled in the book *Kewpies: Dolls and Art of Rose O'Neill and Joseph L. Kallus*. Now, some 18 years later, I have finished another book, this time concentrating on Rose O'Neill's *Kewpies* in all the various forms in which these imps are found. It seems that those who love *Kewpie* love the image in every possible manner in which it was presented—from paper dolls in ladies' magazines from the early years of the 20th century to the little bisque figurines and modern dolls that are currently produced.

It would be a near-impossibility to document in one printed volume every single *Kewpie* form that exists, but a wide general range is presented here. It has been a lot of fun collecting various types of *Kewpies* and photographing them from a few leading collections for a book of collectibles pertaining to *Kewpie* and a few of *Kewpie's* friends. There are many to study and enjoy. We can't each have every *Kewpie* that there is, but it is still rewarding to appreciate them in the form of knowledge.

Chapter 1

Introduction

Rose O'Neill

Rose O'Neill at age 39.

On May 1, 1893, President Grover Cleveland of the United States pressed a button that turned on electric lights and caused motors to run everywhere on the grounds of the World's Columbian Exposition in Chicago. The excited crowd of people who had listened to the President's speech in front of the Administration Building at the fair surged forward. Several women fainted in the crush. Jane Addams, who was later one of the first people to awaken America's social conscience with the opening of Hull House in Chicago in 1899, had her purse snatched. By the time the Exposition had ended on October 31, 1893, more than 27 million people had seen it.

The World's Colombian Exposition had many long-reaching effects: City planning programs, based on the model city at the fair, were imitated especially in Cleveland, Washington and San Francisco. The industrial exhibits at the fair showed how technology would influence the future of citizens around the world. It reaffirmed the American tradition of "progress." Those who attended the Exposition brought home pamphlets, booklets, souvenirs, and literature proclaiming the value of products that are now considered necessities. Those who had been to the fair found that it was an unforgettable experience in their lives. Tons of literature and books were based on the 1893 experience. Even the Elsie Dinsmore books for children celebrated the achievement with a volume in the series called *Elsie at the World's Fair* (1894). Many collectors of various objects, such as coins, tickets, picture books, railroad time schedules, and other things preserve this fascinating era of American history.

The exuberant decade of the 1890s in America was the time of the celebration of the 400th anniversary of the first voyage of Christopher Columbus. The year delay in celebrating Columbus' trip from Spain to the Americas with a World Fair was caused by the immense undertaking of mounting such an enormous exhibit in Chicago. The official reason given was that other American cities would have a chance to have their own local celebrations during 1892.

At any rate, the Columbian Exposition of 1893 was an enormous success. Architects designed a park full of buildings to house the exhibits and displays and many of these buildings had impressive classic facades and porticoes that revived an interest in that style of architecture. Classic motifs in art and decoration became popular once more and Ancient Greece was the inspiration for another romantic movement.

This came at the end of the Victorian era, a time of a new freedom of creativity for both men and women and new expressions in art, literature and design were sought and expressed. The leading centers of intellectual activity were the rapidly growing cities in both Europe and America.

The cosmopolitan life attracted artists and intellectuals and many of them went to Europe to study and to live in sophisticated settings like romantic Paris. Several talented American women were drawn to the Romantic Movement. Gertrude Stein (1874-1946) lived in Paris after 1903 and her home became a center for artists and writers, such as Henri Matisse, Pablo Picasso, Sherwood Anderson, Ezra Pound, Ernest Hemingway, and John Reed. Isadora Duncan (1878-1927) who revolutionized dance by drawing her inspiration from nature, the "god" of the romantics, lived in Europe after 1902. She danced barefoot in a loose tunic, suggested by Greek sculpture, and furthered the 20th century emancipation of women's dress with her unique costumes.

Rose O'Neill's life and work were formed in this same intellectual atmosphere and time. The classical past and the Romantic Movement had a great impact on her creative forces. Rose O'Neill was an illustrator, a

Rose O'Neill by fan Gordon Anderson, 1973.

sculptor, a designer, an artist, a novelist, a poet, and she was a totally original individualist. She was a true modern "Renaissance Woman" who utilized and explored her many talents and interests and left behind a great creative legacy that is still studied and admired almost 130 years after her birth and 60 years after her death.

Of all the many artistic and intellectual accomplishments of Rose O'Neill, the one that will always be best known is her *Kewpie*®. People who have never heard of Rose O'Neill know what the term *Kewpie* implies. Many people still refer to all play dolls as "*Kewpie* dolls." Even a person who does not accurately know what a *Kewpie* looks like knows that it is something very cute and very clever. A current edition of Webster's Dictionary defines *Kewpie* as "...a small chubby doll with a topknot of hair," and does not cite Rose O'Neill. Nude, chubby *Kewpies* with their wry topknots of hair first began as magazine illustrations, but their most popular form has always been dolls and figurines. Everyone loves to look at *Kewpies*; nobody can resist touching and holding a *Kewpie* that is in a modeled form. *Kewpies* amuse and delight and they make one smile. Most of all, they are the artistic expression of a woman who knew how to enjoy life.

True art, whether it is found in literature or in plastic creative mediums, must have excellence of form or expression and it must express ideas of permanent or universal interest. Rose O'Neill's *Kewpies* have met these criteria for close to a century now. Rose O'Neill said her baby brother inspired the creation of *Kewpie* and she stated that

Kewpie was the baby form of Cupid, the Roman god of love. O'Neill declared, "But there is a difference. Cupid gets himself into trouble. The *Kewpies* get themselves out, always searching out ways to make the world better and funnier." This is a great philosophy.

The creator of *Kewpie*, whom so many still revere, was born Cecilia Rose O'Neill on June 25, 1874, in Wilkes-Barre, Pennsylvania. She was the second child of Alice Asenath Cecilia Smith and William Patrick O'Neill, both of whom were talented, creative and artistic. The O'Neills moved to Battle Creek, Nebraska, when Rose was three-years-old. From an early age, Rose's romantically inclined parents instilled in the child their love of classic writers and the myths of the Greek and Roman gods. Rose O'Neill's parents always encouraged her to develop her own creative talents, which included drawing, music and writing.

By the time that Rose was fourteen, the family moved to Omaha, Nebraska, and she had six brothers and sisters. In 1889, Rose entered a drawing contest for children sponsored by the Omaha *World Herald*. Her work was called *Temptation*. It was a rather immodestly clad, for the times, figure of a woman inspired by classical mythology who was fleeing along a rocky path. The drawing was so good that nobody believed it was from the hand of a young girl.

Rose O'Neill paper doll by Gordon Anderson, 1973.

In 1890 Patrick O'Neill inspired Rose to join a company of touring actors to encourage another of her many talents. She was not able to properly interpret the Shakespearean roles that her father loved so much as successfully as they both had hoped so she left the band of strolling players and turned to writing as an outlet for her creative drives. (Reportedly, Rose's father had presented her to Helena Modjeska, the famous 19th century Shakespearean actress, when Rose was about fourteen or fifteen, and Mme. Modjeska informed her that she was too "sensitive" to compete in Modjeska's chosen profession.)

Rose left Omaha and went to New York City in 1893, where she intended to publish a novel she had been working on and to pursue her ambition of drawing illustrations for magazines. Up to that point, she was largely self-taught so she enrolled in art classes and had some success illustrating stories for such magazines as *Truth*, *Harper's Weekly* and *The Great Divide*. Magazine illustration was a field dominated by men at that time so Rose signed her work with her initials "C.R.O." to disguise the fact that she was a woman. The year that Rose left for New York, her father moved his

Rose O'Neill paper doll by Gordon Anderson, 1973.

family to a rural setting in the southern Ozark Mountains in Missouri. The O'Neills called their new home "Bonniebrook." Bonniebrook, which was basically a rustic cabin at that time, eventually had a great influence on Rose O'Neill and it affected the rest of her life. The pastoral serenity of Bonniebrook appealed to Rose's romantic nature and the tranquility of living in a remote district allowed her more time to formulate her future creative visions.

Gray Latham, a young man whom Rose had met while the family was living in Omaha, became her suitor while she was staying at Bonniebrook. He and Rose were married in 1896. Rose returned to New York with Latham and worked as an illustrator for *Puck* magazine, signing her drawings "O'Neill-Latham." Gray Latham appeared as a male model in many of Rose's works at this time. Sadly, Rose's marriage to Latham was not a happy one. In 1901, Rose and Latham were divorced and she returned again to Bonniebrook to renew her spirit. Rose continued her career as a magazine illustrator.

Rose married Harry Leon Wilson, *Puck's* literary editor, about a year after she returned to Bonniebrook. Both Rose and Wilson resigned their positions with *Puck* and moved to Connecticut to work at writing novels. In 1904, Rose's first book, *The Loves of Edwy*, was published. Wilson published the classic novels *Ruggles of Red Gap* and *Merton of the Movies*, among others. By 1930, Rose had published three more adult novels—*The Lady in the White Veil* (1909), *Garda* (1929) and *The Goblin Woman* (1930). In 1922, she did a book of poetry, *The Master Mistress.* During this period she also authored four children's books. They were *The Kewpies and Dottie Darling* (1910), *The Kewpies, Their Book* (1912), *The Kewpie Primer* (1912), and *The Kewpies and the Runaway Baby* (1928). The Wilsons were close friends of Pulitzer Prize-winning novelist Booth Tarkington and his poetess wife. Rose also did illustrations for the Tarkingtons' literary works. In 1905, the Wilsons and the Tarkingtons spent the summer in Italy at a villa on the Isle of Capri, where Mr. Wilson and Mr. Tarkington co-wrote the successful Broadway play *The Man From Home.*

After five years as the wife of Harry Leon Wilson, the outgoing and vivacious Rose became disillusioned with Wilson's moods of despair and silence and she divorced him. They reportedly remained supportive friends afterwards.

Once again Rose O'Neill returned to Bonniebrook in the Ozarks. Supposedly, she was melancholy because of the disappointments in her life and she became more introspective and reflective. While she was at Bonniebrook she claimed that little elfin creatures appeared to her in a dream. She reported in the *Woman's Home Companion* in January 1914 that

> ...They were all on my bedspread, hopping about, or sitting along the bed frame at the foot like a row of chickadees.
>
> They were extremely lively and as hard to count as is a brood of little chickens; as they bounced from fold to fold of my counterpane I saw their topknots waving. ...They seemed to be about eight inches high, and as far as I could see, their noses were no more than dots...And so I have ever since faithfully portrayed them.
>
> In my childhood, I had loved the *Brownies* of Mr. Palmer Cox, and one of the delightful things about them was that one always reposed on the feeling that, whatever they did, they "meant well" by it. So the *Kewpies*, who I have liked to think might be young toddling cousins of that earlier illustrious family. A *Kewpie* meeting a *Brownie,* I'm sure, would be almost overcome with respect.

Rose drew pictures of these little creatures with plump nude bodies and a small topknot of hair. For several years she had drawn similar chubby little babies for her illustration work. The elf-like creatures who visited Rose O'Neill in her dreams first appeared as magazine illustrations for *The Ladies' Home Journal* in December of 1909. These charming little imps became popular immediately and Rose was commissioned to create them for various publications and for advertisements. This was the beginning of *Kewpie*®.

Very quickly *Kewpie* became big business for Rose O'Neill and the demand for various forms of *Kewpie* was overwhelming. Within a short period of time, *Kewpie* appeared in every possible medium from drawings and illustrations to dolls and figurines in various forms and materials. In 1913, Rose O'Neill obtained a copyright for her very original and unique little character. Almost one hundred years later, the craze still exists for Rose O'Neill's *Kewpies* in all forms, especially among collectors.

By 1912, Geo. Borgfeldt & Co. of New York, a distributor of dolls, toys and novelties, had become interested in marketing a line of *Kewpie* figurines and dolls. For this project, the Borgfeldt Company and Rose required the assistance of additional artists and sculptors. An advertisement was sent to the Fine Arts College of Pratt Institute in Brooklyn. Interested young artists who could draw and sculpt children were asked to present themselves to Fred Kolb of Borgfeldt and apply for the position of developing a line of *Kewpie* merchandise.

Joseph Kallus of Brooklyn, a young student who was studying at Pratt Institute on a scholarship, was selected for the *Kewpie* project after Rose O'Neill had approved his work. Borgfeldt planned to produce dolls and figurines in Germany, where the company had affiliates and where porcelain production, which requires a great deal of hand finishing, was more economical than in the United States.

Rose O'Neill's younger sister Callista was studying art in Italy at this time. Rose traveled to Europe to encourage Callista to be her business manager and to help oversee production of *Kewpies* abroad. While she was in Italy, Rose went to Capri to visit Charles Caryl Coleman, a friend of her father, who owned the Villa Narcissus. Coleman, an elderly and wealthy artist, was captivated by the young, beautiful and vivacious Rose and reportedly wanted to make her the inheritor of his Italian properties. To avoid entangling Italian inheritance laws, Rose purchased the Villa Narcissus from Coleman for a modest sum. Coleman and his staff continued to live in the villa until his death in 1929 at age ninety-six. He left Rose his collection of paintings and art treasures which he had acquired during his long life.

By 1918, because of the dangers of World War I in Europe, Rose and Callista returned to the United States and shared an apartment at 61

Washington Square in New York. In the meantime, Rose continued to submit her *Kewpie* drawings and poems to *Woman's Home Companion* and *Good Housekeeping.* These and other projects and the royalties from *Kewpie* dolls and figurines made Rose O'Neill wealthy. Her income permitted her to remodel Bonniebrook in Missouri into a comfortable fourteen-room house.

Rose began to express a unique personal taste in her manner of dress by this time. She now preferred to wear flowing gowns made of filmy materials, such as she had seen in artwork from Classical Greece while in Europe. (This was also the style of Isadora Duncan at the time.) At her apartment on Washington Square, she entertained other artists, writers and intellectuals whose company she enjoyed. During this period, the popular song *Rose of Washington Square* was written by Ballard McDonald with music by James F. Hanlery and copyrighted by Shaprio, Bernstein & Co. in 1919. Rose O'Neill experts feel that the creator of *Kewpie* was the inspiration for this popular tune, which has long been associated with comedienne Fanny Brice. (*Rose of Washington Square* was the theme song of the 1939 film of the same title, which was a thinly disguised version of the life story of Fanny Brice.)

In 1919, Rose became good friends with a Norwegian couple, Matta and Berger Lie, who were visiting the United States on a business trip. Rose showed the Lies her newest drawings, which she called her "Sweet Monsters." These Monster drawings were a series of voluptuous and sensuous nude figures, including fauns, satyrs, centaurs, and other mythical creatures, executed in pen and ink. Later, some of these drawings were translated into large sculptures, such as *The Embrace of the Tree,* which Rose installed at Bonniebrook. The Lies encouraged Rose to do more work based on these sorts of themes and invited her to come to Norway where they would provide her with a studio to produce more pagan-like renderings. Rose and Callista traveled to Norway and remained with Matta and Berger Lie for about six months.

After visiting with the Lies, Rose traveled to Paris and enrolled in a course at the studio of the recently deceased French artist Auguste Rodin (1840-1917). Rodin was considered the most important sculptor of his time. Rose's Monster drawings show a great deal of kinship to such Rodin works as *The Thinker* and *Adam and Eve.* Her Monster drawings were exhibited in Paris and later at the Wildenstein Gallery in New York.

While Rose was in Paris, she began private instructions in the French language with Jeanne Galeron and then with Galeron's younger brother, Jean. Jean Galeron returned to America with Rose and lived at Bonniebrook for a while and then settled in New York with Callista's help. (There were rumors that Rose had married the much younger French artist, but she neither confirmed nor denied these reports. Jean Galeron later married an English girl in Los Angeles.)

During the 1920s, Rose O'Neill lived well from the profits of her work. She was the highest paid woman illustrator of the time; she was a world traveler; she had well-known friends in the art world in several countries; and she was active in the movement for Women's Suffrage, producing posters and drawings for the cause. During this period, she bought a home in Connecticut that she named Carabas Castle.

At Carabas Castle, Rose sculpted her newest creation, *Scootles,* the little traveler who "scooted" all over the world. Scootles was always more popular in doll form than any other medium, unlike *Kewpie* who was produced in all media and materials.

In 1937, Rose, who was now sixty-three years old, sold Carabas Castle and her Washington Square town house and returned home to Bonniebrook in Missouri. She continued to work on new artistic projects and to promote her popular ones, such as *Kewpie.* She even negotiated with a movie studio in Hollywood to produce a film featuring *Kewpie,* but this project never reached fruition. One of her new creations at Bonniebrook was *Ho-Ho,* the little laughing Buddha doll that caused an adverse reaction from Buddhists when it was mass-produced later.

Rose O'Neill died in Springfield, Missouri, at the home of a nephew on April 6, 1944, after having suffered several strokes. She was buried at her beloved Bonniebrook in the family plot alongside her mother and her brother James. Callista died in 1946. Bonniebrook burned to the ground in 1947 because of a faulty heating stove.

Before her death, Rose O'Neill gave some of her artwork to the museum of The School of the Ozarks (a college) in Point Lookout, Missouri. The museum of the School of the Ozarks also houses an extensive collection of Rose O'Neill memorabilia, such as *Kewpie* dolls, Rose O'Neill's original artwork and copies of her books.

Dr. Bruce Trimble and his wife Mary preserved other Rose O'Neill memorabilia pertaining to her life particularly those associated with her years at Bonniebrook. In 1946, the Trimbles purchased a farm near Branson, Missouri, which is not far from Bonniebrook. This farm was the setting of Harold Bell Wright's popular and sentimental novel *The Shepherd of the Hills*. The Trimbles established a museum at the Shepherd of the Hills Farm and in the Rose O'Neill Room they exhibited all the artifacts pertaining to her work that they had managed to collect.

Collectors of Rose O'Neill material have done even more to preserve her memory and her work. Although figurines and dolls of *Kewpie* were first produced as inexpensive novelty items, a vast number of them have been kept in excellent condition and are still seen for sale on the collectors' market. Many enthusiasts have huge collections focusing on the designs of Rose O'Neill. Pearl Hodges of Branson, Missouri, who promoted Rose O'Neill Week to honor the creator of *Kewpie*, first organized the Rose O'Neill collectors in 1967. This led to the formation of the National and International Rose O'Neill Clubs, with several affiliates, the largest of which is the California Rose O'Neill Association.

Each year Branson, Missouri, hosts the annual Rose O'Neill Kewpiesta to promote and preserve the memory of Rose O'Neill and her *Kewpies*. The International Rose O'Neill Club has sponsored such efforts as archeological digs at the site of Bonniebrook to search for *Kewpie* parts and other items that may have survived the fire of 1947. In 1974, the admirers of Rose O'Neill encouraged the governor of Missouri, Christopher S. Bond, to proclaim June 25, 1974, as Rose O'Neill Day in honor of the great Missourian's 100th birthday. Jean Cantwell reported on this event in the *Antique Trader Weekly* of August 27, 1974, and successfully described the day:

> One hundred years after her birth, the charm, beauty, and ethereal love of Rose O'Neill still permeates the land where she perceived the *Kewpies* and captured them, with love, on her easel.

The National Rose O'Neill Club of Branson, Missouri, also publishes a biannual *Kewpiesta Kourier*, which is sent to members "to preserve and cherish the memory of Rose O'Neill and to inform the public about her and her works."

Audrey Looman, the current president of IROC (The International Rose O'Neill Club), which was founded as a commemorative to honor Rose O'Neill, told me recently of one of the objectives of this organization: IROC recognizes the importance of offering education to people who have just discovered Rose O'Neill and her *Kewpies*. This organization is also dedicated to the importance of the continued restoration and conservation of Bonniebrook.

The true genius of Rose O'Neill was best exemplified by her ability to seek out or to attract others who inspired her and encouraged her to pursue her artistic and creative endeavors. It is also seen in the love that many thousands of persons have had over the years for her work and for herself as a truly unique woman. If Rose O'Neill had never done anything else except to draw *Kewpies*, she would be still be acknowledged as an important creative talent whose works and designs would always be a part of America's artistic heritage.

Rose O'Neill's philosophy was, "Do good deeds in a funny way. The world needs to laugh, or at least to smile more than it does."

Original postcards from circa 1912 from the Gibson Art Company, Cincinnati. Each one is "signed" by Rose O'Neill. *Karen Shaker Collection.*

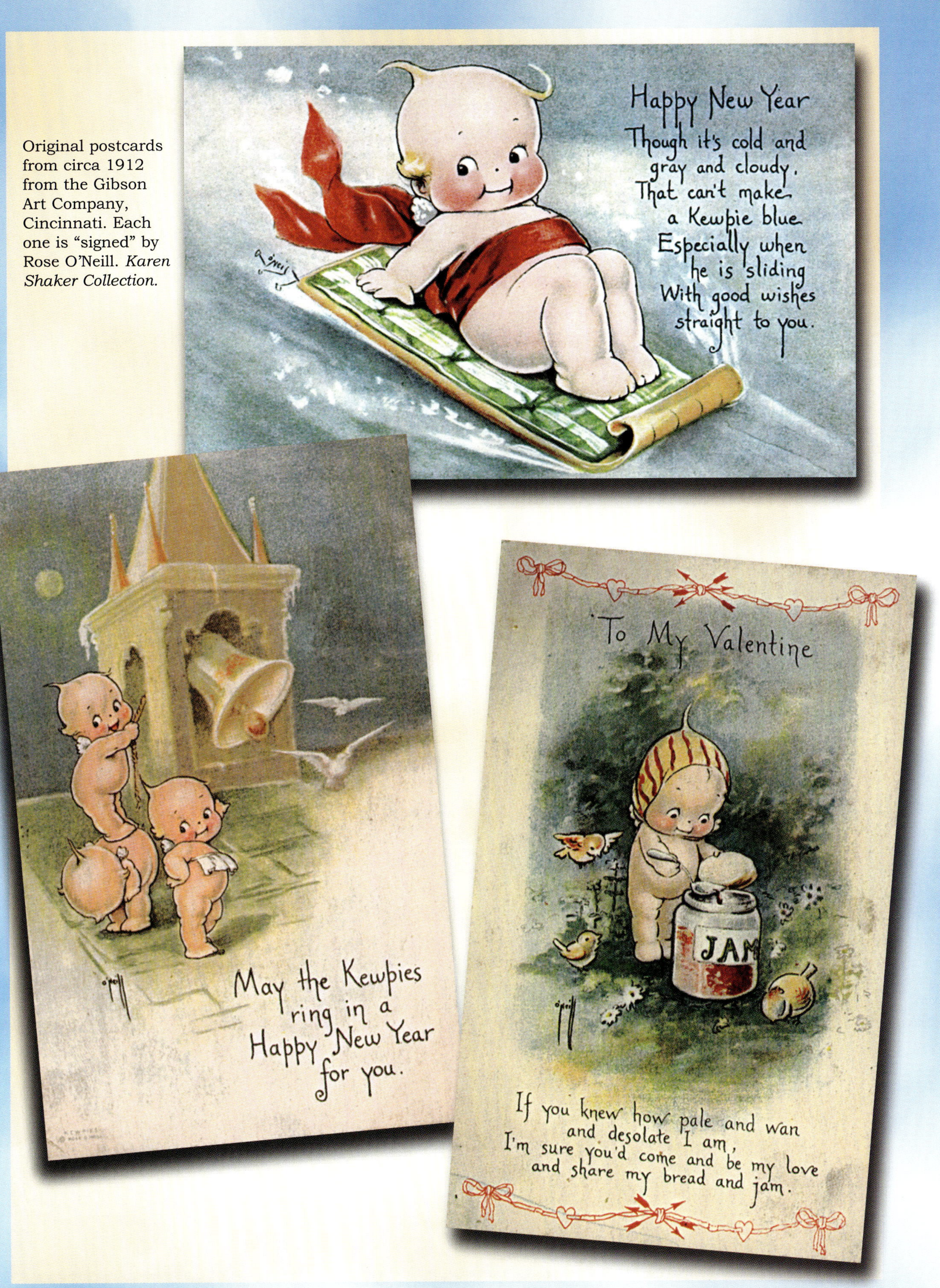

Happy New Year
Though it's cold and gray and cloudy,
That can't make a Kewpie blue
Especially when he is sliding
With good wishes straight to you.
May the Kewpies ring in a Happy New Year for you.
To My Valentine
JAM
If you knew how pale and wan and desolate I am,
I'm sure you'd come and be my love and share my bread and jam.

Said Romeo Kewpie
to sweet Juliet
"I hope you're as happy
as can be, you bet,"
And that's just what I say
In the same fervent way.
'Cause I hope you are
happy on Valentine's Day.

Can't think of
an earthly thing
to say,
'Cept I hope you are
happy
Valentine's Day.

Two cute little Kewpies
To greet you and say
How much joy
I am wishing you
Valentine's Day.

Original postcards from circa 1912 from the Gibson Art Company, Cincinnati. Each one is "signed" by Rose O'Neill. *Karen Shaker Collection.*

Please tack this notice
on your door
So everyone can see
I've picked you out
from all the world
My Valentine to be.

DEAREST
YOU ARE MY VALENTINE
YOURS RESPECTFULLY
KEWPIE
KEWPIES
©ROSE O'NEILL

Original postcards from circa 1912 from the Gibson Art Company, Cincinnati. Each one is "signed" by Rose O'Neill. *Karen Shaker Collection.*

Can't kneel to you as Kewpies do
And tell my thoughts
so kind and true,
But I can say
In cordial way
I hope you are happy
This Valentine's Day

These jolly Kewpies

"How-do-you-do,"
and wish you

Easter season.

I send a Kewpie here to do
A little Christmas chore or two
See him prepare
The Yule-log there
While I am wishing skies of blue:
And the gladdest year of all for you.

Original postcards from circa 1912 from the Gibson Art Company, Cincinnati. Each one is "signed" by Rose O'Neill. *Karen Shaker Collection.*

There's a bit of good luck
in the box for you.
For everybody knows
That the Kewpies come
from Fairyland
The place where
good luck grows.

If you want to make me happy

Just pack your grip
And take that trip
To come and visit me.

Original postcards from circa 1915 from Gartner & Bender Publs., Chicago. These pictures do not credit Rose O'Neill and are only marked "© G&B." *Karen Shaker Collection.*

LETTER BOX
U.S. MAIL
Was glad to get that letter from you,
I sat right down and read it thru;
If it was longer, I'd like it better,
However I'll answer soon with a letter.

INK
©G&B
Several times I've tried to write,
And I think and think with all my might;
So I send you this to let you know
That I'm thinking of you so.

© G&B
A little bird told me something,
And I hope that it comes true;
He said that very soon I'd get
A letter sent by you.

© G&B
I wish I had a motor car,
Do you know what I would do?
I'd jump right in
And take a spin
As fast as I could to you.

Original postcards from circa 1915 from Gartner & Bender Publs., Chicago. These pictures do not credit Rose O'Neill and are only marked "© G&B." *Karen Shaker Collection.*

© G&B
What's the matter? Anything wrong?
Seems that I've waited awful long
For some news of you, my friend,
Where's the word you promised to send?

Part of a large series of reproduction cards from the 1970s by Baker Mktg. Co. of Missouri. These are taken from original Rose O'Neill art by Florence Baker. The set is called "Kewpieville." No copyright credits are given. Note the card that shows one of Palmer Cox's *Brownies. Shirley Karaba Collection.*

JALE
Rose o'Neill

GRAND KEWPIEVILLE HOTEL
Rules and Regulations.
Any Guest not having a good time will be reported to the Management.
Room, Clerk.

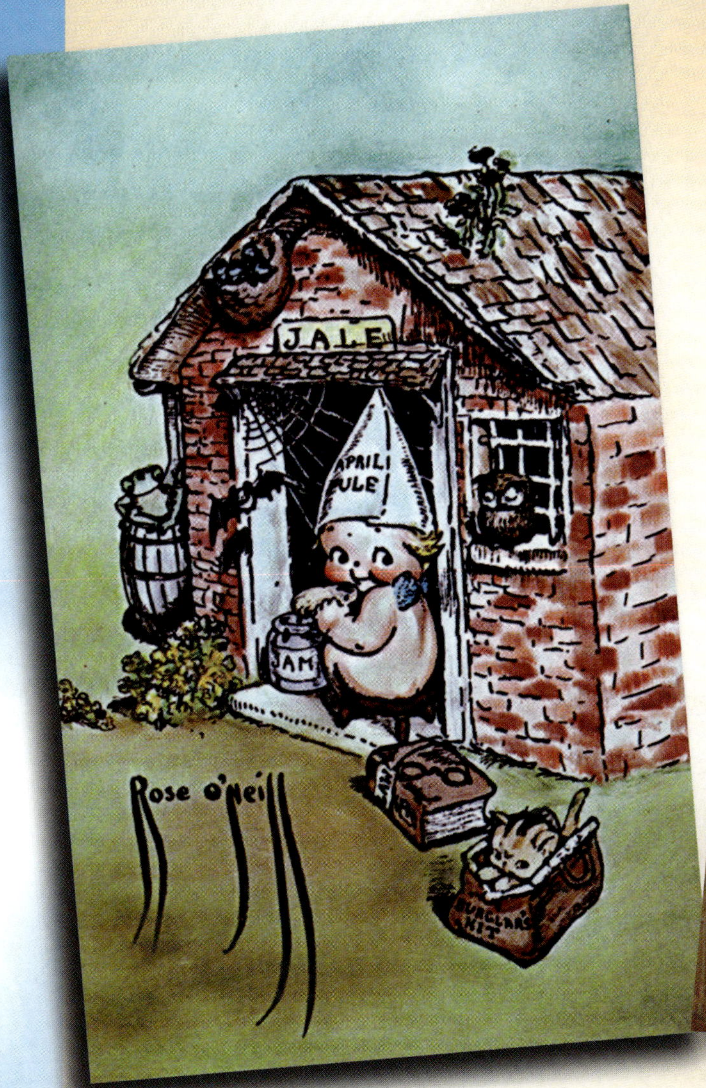

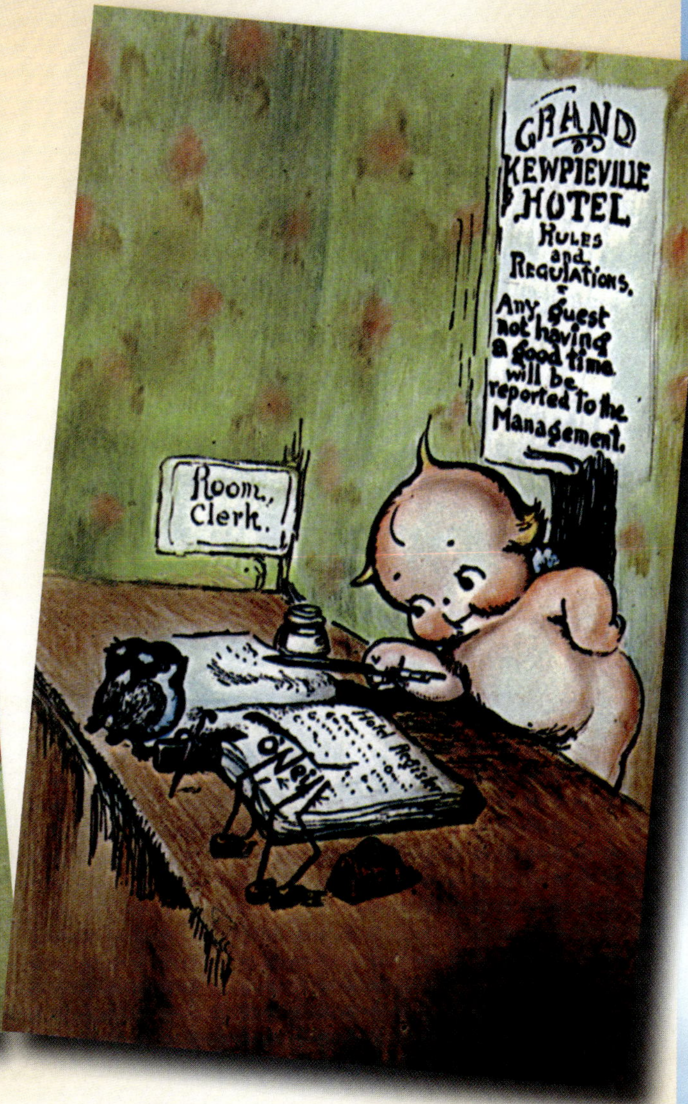

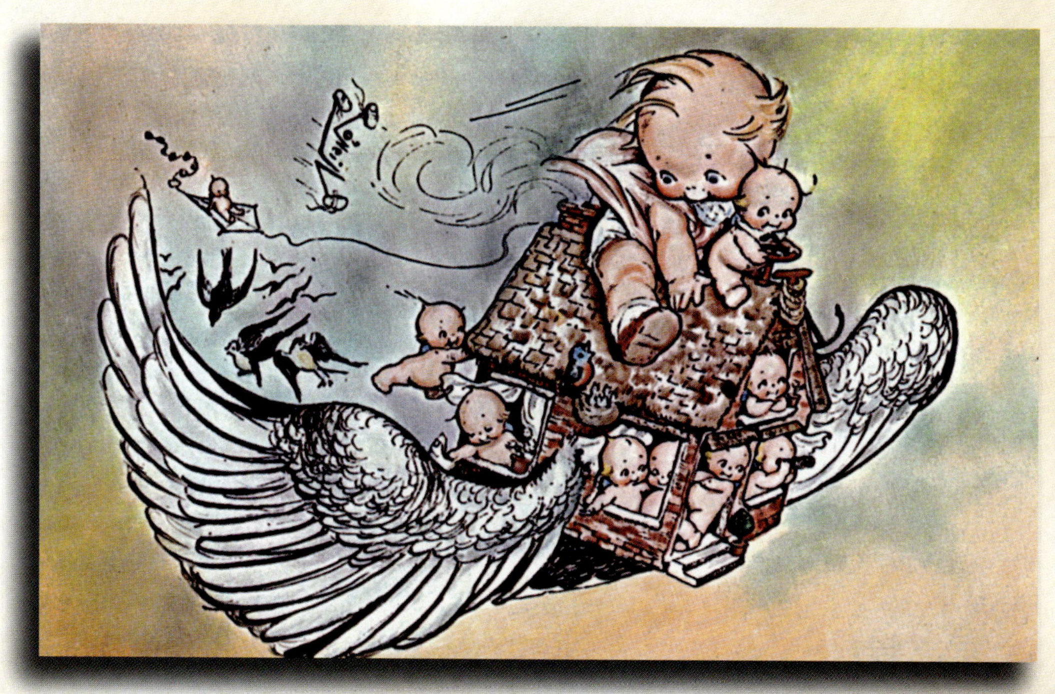

More cards from the large series of reproduction cards by Florence Baker taken from original Rose O'Neill art. The 1970s cardset by Baker Mktg. Co. of Missouri is called "Kewpieville" and gives no copyright credit. *Shirley Karaba Collection.*

The Kewpies Tidying

Reproduction cards from the 1970s taken from original art "owned by the Ashers" and "owned by the Drays." No copyright credits are given. *Shirley Karaba Collection.*

The Kewpies Eating

These cards, capitalizing on America's Bicentennial (1976), were "adapted by artist Florence Baker" from original Rose O'Neill postcards of the 1910s. No copyright credits are given. *Shirley Karaba Collection.*

1776 - 1976
Bicentennial
Rose O'Neill
by Florence Baker
Our First Flag

Bicentennial
1776 - 1976
Rose O'Neill
by Florence Baker
Crossing the Delaware
Bicentennial
1776 - 1976
Rose O'Neill
by Florence Baker
The Spirit of '76

Magazine Pages

Most of the magazine pages featuring *Kewpies* were printed in black and white with pinkish tints on some elements in the drawings. Full-pages in color, most of which were the *Kewpie Kutouts*, were in the *Woman's Home Companion* from October 1912 through February 1914. This magazine and *The Ladies' Home Journal* and *The Delineator* were large format magazines at the time the *Kewpies* were featured in them.

Good Housekeeping was about the same size format that most magazines are today. The titles of the *Kewpie* articles are listed. They were mostly "verses with pictures" by Rose O'Neill with the exception of the "Kutouts" and were from one to four pages in length. Other types of Rose O'Neill articles are cited with the respective listing. The *Kewpie* stories in verse were meant "for younger readers" and were usually listed as such.

	The Ladies' Home Journal
December 1909	*The Kewpies' Christmas Frolic*
January 1910	*The Kewpies and the Aeroplane*
February 1910	*The Kewpies and the Baby*
December 15, 1910	*The Children's Annual with a color cover by Rose O'Neill*
April 1925 – January 1928	*Kewpieville* (monthly verse and pictures)
December 1927	*Kewpie Christmas Cover*
	Woman's Home Companion
September 1910	*Dotty Darling and the Kewpies ...a Circus*
October 1910	*Dotty Darling and the Kewpies ...at School*
November 1910	*Dotty Darling and the Kewpies ...Thanksgiving*
December 1910	*Dotty Darling and the Kewpies ...The Kewpies' Christmas Tree*
January 1911	*Dotty Darling and the Kewpies ...Timely Cheer*
February 1911	*Dotty's Kewpish Valentine*
March 1911	*Dotty Darling and the Kewpies ...The Kewpies Taught Our Dot to Fly*
April 1911	*Dotty Darling and the Kewpies ...How the Kewps Met Dotty's Baby*
June 1911	*Dotty Darling and the Kewpies ...The Kewpies Save Dot's Baby*
July 1911	*How the Kewps Gave Dot a Trip*
October 1911	*The Kewpies and Their New Adventures*
November 1911	*The Kewpies and Dotty Darling*
December 1911	*The Kewpies' Christmas Party*
January 1912	*The Kewpies and the McGraws*
February 1912	*The Kindly Kewpies*
March 1912	*The Kewpies and the Scolding Aunt*
April 1912	*The Kewpies and Jim McGrew*
May 1912	*The Kewpies and the Dismal Grumps*
June 1912	*The Kewpies and the Circus*

	***Woman's Home Companion* (continued)**
July 1912	*The Kewpies and the Little Browns*
August 1912	*The Kewpies and the Poor Old Soul*
September 1912	*The Kewpies' Plan*
October 1912	Color Cover by Rose O'Neill The first of the *Kewpie Kutouts* Full page ad for *Kewpie Kutouts* The paper *Kewpies*
November 1912	The *Kewpie Kutouts—The Kewpie Cook and Dotty Darling's Mother*
December 1912	*Stern Irene and the Kewpie Gardner (Kewpie Kutouts)* *The Kewps and Stern Irene*
January 1913	The *Kewpie Kutouts—The One That's Careful of His Voice and Dotty Darling's Sister Nan* *The Kewpies and Sister Nan*
February 1913	The *Kewpie Kutouts—The One Who Always Wears His Overshoes and Dotty Darling's Brother Dan* *The Kewpies and Brother Dan*
March 1913	The *Kewpie Kutouts—The Kewpie Army and the Orphan Boy* *The Kewpies and the Orphan Boy*
April 1913	*The Kewpies and Father Darling*
May 1913	*The Flying Kewpies*—A New and Fascinating Kewpish Family (front and back *Kewpies* to glue together) *How the Kewps Turned into Dolls*
June 1913	The *Kewpie Kutouts—Little Assunta and Her Kewpie Doll* *Little Assunta and the Kewpie Doll*
July 1913	*Dotty and Four of Her Kewpie Friends* (paper doll/front and back *Kewpies*) *The Kewpies and Little Samuel*
August 1913	*The Musical Kewpies and the Little German Girl* (paper doll/front and back *Kewpies*) *The Kewpies and the Little German Girl*
September 1913	*The Wealthy Kewpie and the Wealthy Child* (paper doll/front and back *Kewpie*) *The Kewpies and the Wealthy Child*
October 1913	*The Kewpie Nurse and the Better Baby* (paper doll/front and back *Kewpie*) *The Kewpies and the Better Baby*
December 1913	*The Kewpie Dog and the Bad Little Boy* (front and back boy, dog, *Kewpie*) *The Kewpie Christmas Dog*
January 1914	*Flying Kewpies—Who Want to Fly About Your Christmas Tree* (front and back *Kewpies*) *The Kewpies and Santa Claus*
February 1914	*A Kewpie Valentine* (project) *The Kewpies and Little Peggy*
March 1914	*Kewpies on Parade* (sheet music with Rose O'Neill *Kewpie* art)

	Good Housekeeping
May 1914	*The Kewpies are Coming*
June 1914	*The Kewpies Arrive*
July 1914	*The Kewpies and Ducky Daddles*
August 1914	*The Kewpies and Tibby's Tree*
September 1914	*The Kewpies and the Young McShanes*
October 1914	*The Kewpies and Bedtime*
November 1914	*The Kewpies and Thanksgiving*
December 1914	*The Kewpies on Christmas Eve*
January 1915	*The Kewpies and Old Father Time*
February 1915	*The Kewpies and Miss Susan*
March 1915	*The Kewpies and Sad Little Sammy*
April 1915	*The Kewpish Adventures of the Kewpidoodle*
May 1915	*The Kewpies and Ducky Daddles*
June 1915	*Tom, Dick & Harry Meet the Kewpies*
July 1915	*The Kewpies and Little Petie*
August 1915	*The Kewpies and the Ancient Mariner*
September 1915	*The Kewpies and Samuel Grudge*
October 1915	*The Kewpies and Little Hieronimous*
November 1915	*The Kewpies and the Rainy Day*
December 1915	*The Kewpies and Santa Claus*
January 1916	*The Kewpies and the Blizzard*
February 1916	*The Kewpies and the Twins*
March 1916	*The Kewpies and Proud Peter*
April 1916	*The Kewpies and Tommy Todd*
May 1916	*The Kewpies and Matilda's Aunt*
June 1916	*The Kewpies and Farmer Brown*
July 1916	*The Kewpies and their Fairy Cousin*
August 1916	*The Kewpies and the Cannibal*
September 1916	*The Kewpies and Young Nimrod*
October 1916	*The Kewpies and the College*
November 1916	*The Kewpies and Thanksgiving*
December 1916	*The Kewpies and Little Johnny Smith*
January 1917	*The Kewpies and the Procrastinating Prissy*

	***Good Housekeeping* (continued)**
February 1917	*The Kewpies and Washington's Birthday*
March 1917	*The Kewpies and Little Samantha*
April 1917	*The Kewpies and the Deserted Farm*
May 1917	*The Kewpies and Active Artie*
June 1917	*The Kewpies and the Pleasant Princess*
July 1917	*The Kewpies and the Fairy Child*
August 1917	*The Kewpies and the Goblin*
September 1917	*The Kewpies and the Little Mermaid*
October 1917	*How the Kewpies Played Baby*
November 1917	*The Kewpies and Little Susie*
December 1917	*The Kewpies and the Forgotten Toys*
January 1918	*The Kewpies and Their Winter Industry*
February 1918	*The Kewpies and the Calendar*
March 1918	*The Kewpies and their School of Jollity*
April 1918	*The Kewpies and April Fool's Day*
May 1918	*The Kewpies and the Invalid Girl*
June 1918	*The Kewpies at the Sea Shore*
July 1918	*The Kewpies and Liberty's Birthday*
August 1918	*The Kewpies and Dusty Dan*
September 1918	*The Kewpies and Food Preservation*
October 1918	*The Kewpies Prepare for Winter*
November 1918	*The Kewpies and the Cold Princess*
December 1918	*The Kewpies and their Great Christmas Idea*
January 1919	*The Kewpies and Midwinter*
February 1919	*The Kewpies and the Proud Children*
March 1919	*The Kewpies and Baby Jones*
April 1919	*The Kewpies That Wanted to Be a Real Baby*
May 1919	*The Kewpies and the Haunted House*
June 1919	*The Kewpies and the Sad Fairy*
July 1919	*The Kewpies and the Glorious Fourth*
	The Delineator
May 1928 – September 1928	*The Kewpies* (monthly page)

Magazine cover, December 15, 1910.

The Rose O'Neill series "Dotty Darling and the Kewpies" began in the *Woman's Home Companion* in September 1910. The stories in verse with drawings by Rose O'Neill were accompanied with the "*Kewpie* Kutouts" from October 1912 through February 1914, although the later ones were not designated as "Kutouts." The "Kutouts" and projects were all printed in full-color, a rarity in magazines during the 1910s. At this time the *Woman's Home Companion* was 16in (41cm) in height. All these pages are from the *Shirley Karaba Collection.*

October 1910. "The Pleasing Tale of Dotty and the Kewpies at School."

DOTTY DARLING AND THE KEWPIES

The Pleasing Tale of Dotty and the Kewpies at School

The Second Kewpie Story
With Verses and Pictures

BY ROSE O'NEILL

Dear children, if you feel inclined
For stories of the Kewpish kind,
Here's one that's really quite amazing;
In fact, perhaps a little dazing.
Some folk insist it isn't true,
I've said 'twas plain as two and two,
I've argued till my face was blue.
I've argued straight with reasons sound,

"Pell-mell they scampered, trotting, pacing, Never stopping, hopping, racing"

And then I've argued 'round and 'round.
I've often argued half the night
Till it was clear as black and white
And mathematically right.
But still they said it wasn't true,
And so I'll leave the thing to you.
(And here's the story exactly as I heard it.)

'Twas in the month of mild October
When little children, calm and sober,
Each morning saunter off to schools,
Respecting all the laws and rules.
The Darling family each morning
Finished washing and adorning,
And down the hill, like children good,
Went off to school with promptitude.
That is, the eldest three, I mean,
Dan, Nan, and stately, stern Irene.
But as for little Dot, poor dear,
'Twas very sad for her, I fear.
Still kept at home and left behind,
When for the school she fairly pined
With longing to improve her mind.
Of course, she toddled after freely.
Poor child! She couldn't help it, really—
Of course, they ran; of course, they fled.
They told her to go home to bed;
They left her toddling past the shed.
Pell-mell they scampered,
trotting,
pacing,
Never stopping,
hopping,
racing,
Down the hill with prancing plunges,
Jiggling books and slates and sponges.
(Oh, so hastily!)

One day, the Kewpies, chancing near,
Beheld this treatment of the dear.
"Look," cried the Kewpie Carpenter,
"The child we made the circus fer!"
As soon as Dot descried the crew,
Her tears were dried like morning dew.
"Oh, take me to the school!" she cried.
"Exactly so," the Chief replied.
"Let all your troubles be removed,
Your mind shall be at once improved.
Although, I think there is a rule
That Kewpies must not go to school;
For Kewps, you know, are such a rarity
They're apt to rouse a slight hilarity.
But come along, sweet Dot, with me;
Like Mary's Lamb, we'll go and see."
(A sensible idea!)

Well, language fails! I don't know *how*
To tell of all that happened now!
Imagine how the children smile,
As all these Kewps go up the aisle!
The dropping slates, the dropping books!
Imagine how the teacher looks!
Imagine how Irene and Nan
Stare open-mouthed (and so does Dan)
To see the child they left so droopy
Come to school beside a Kewpie.

"The other Kewpies calm and mild Each seats himself beside a child"

The Chief sits down beside the dear
And starts to study, whispering clear.
Upon the harder words they linger,
And point them out with studious finger.
The other Kewpies calm and mild,
Each seats himself beside a child,
At which, each child with joy and pride,
Can hardly keep its bliss inside.
(Oh, dear! If I had one by me,
I'd nearly die of jollity!)
Then with the children they recite.
Some Kewps upon the blackboard write,

"The seacher looked in blank surprise"

Thanks to their wings, at quite a height.
The Kewpie Cook spells "pot" and "kettle,"
The Carpenter is on his mettle;
When "Teacher" does for silence shout,
He hammers loud to help her out.
The Kewpie Army then spells "guns,"
At which, the Kewpie Cook spells "buns."
The Kewpie Farmer's good at verbs
Because he thinks that they are herbs.
Sweet Dot is pleased they do so well,
And proud to hear them count and spell.
(They acquit themselves so creditably.)

But, oh, the teacher! Dear! she seems
Quite like a person lost in dreams!
She looks at them in blank surprise,
As if she can't believe her eyes;
And when the afternoon is done,
The Army fires his little gun,
Both Kewps and children hurry out
With many a whoop and laughing shout,
And little feet that whirl about.

"Some Kewps upon the blackboard write"

The teacher says, "My! I must take
A tonic!" with a pinch and shake
To see if she is quite awake.
While Nan and Dan and tall Irene
Said, "Such a thing I've *never* seen!"
(And I'm sure they never had.)
But nothing troubled Dotty's head
That night as she was put to bed.
She felt the little Kewps were kind
And much improvement in her mind.

Front cover by Rose O'Neill, October 1912.

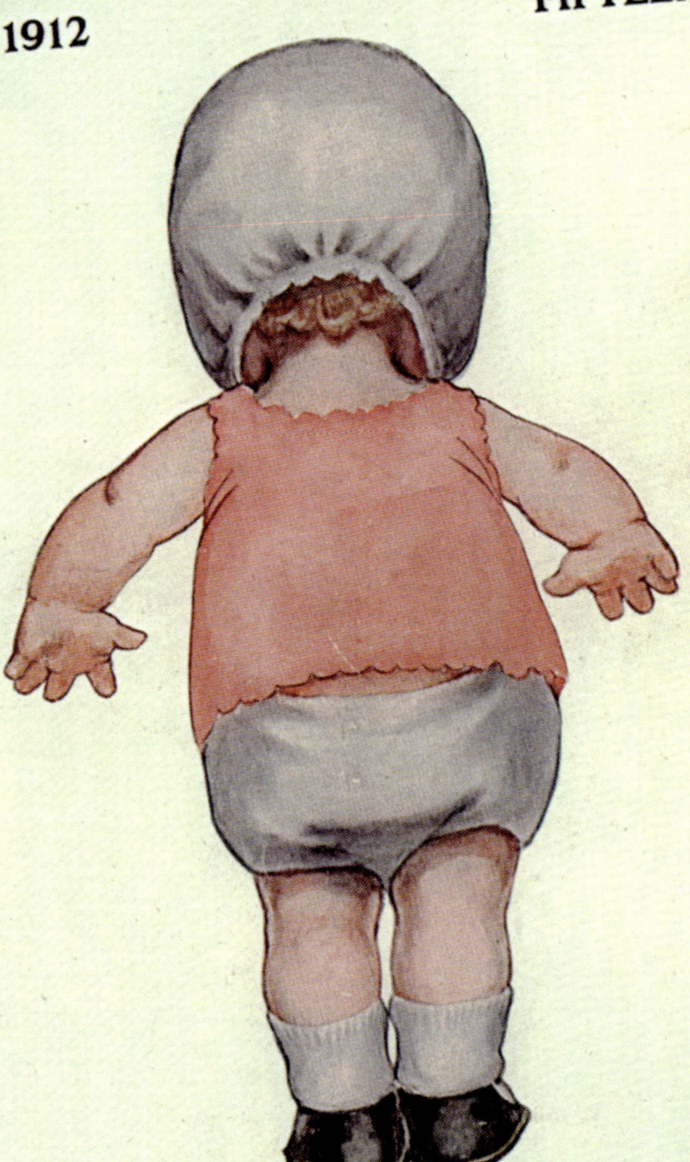

This page is for Children
Kewpie Kutouts
in Many Colors
Every month in Woman's Home Companion
PASTE
THE Kewpies were invented by Rose O'Neill. They are always doing good, helping Dotty Darling and her Baby Brother to have a good time whenever the older children wouldn't let them tag along. Now all the children want to cut out the Kewpies. And the Kewpies want to be cut out by the children. So Rose O'Neill has made the Kewpie Kutouts. There is a whole page of them for you in the October copy of the Woman's Home Companion—a magazine with pages and pages for children and their mothers.
Wag, the Chief—his back
Wag, the Chief
This is Wag, the Chief. He is captain of the band of Kewpies that have been making things so pleasant for Very Little Folks, whose mothers take the Woman's Home Companion. When you cut him out and paste him together, he makes a real Kewpie whichever way you look at him.
Dotty Darling is over five inches high in the Kewpie Kutout.
Dotty's Baby Brother is not quite so tall as Dotty, because he is younger.
The Kewpies are the first cutouts to have real backs.
In October Woman's Home Companion you will find Wag in color (not plain black and white like he is here) and Dotty Darling (with two dresses) and Dotty's Baby Brother all ready to be cut out.
A delicious story about Dotty Darling and her Kewpies has a page all to itself opposite the Kewpie Kutouts.
Ask your Mother for 15 cents
—then hurry to a news-stand and buy the October Woman's Home Companion, which has the first of the Kewpie Kutouts, or send the 15 cents to us right away with your name and address on the Kewpie Kupon. We will send you by return mail the October Woman's Home Companion, postage paid.
WOMAN'S HOME COMPANION
at 381 Fourth Avenue, New York
"Use this Kupon"
Woman's Home Companion
381 Fourth Ave., New York
Here is my 15c. Please send me right away the October Woman's Home Companion containing the first of the Kewpie Kutouts.
Name
Address

October 1912. Advertisement to encourage children to purchase the magazine.

October 1912.

Page 42 WOMAN'S HOME COMPANION October, 1912

The Paper Kewpies

Verses and Pictures

By Rose O'Neill

This tells the Kewpies' latest caper,
With Kewpie dolls cut out of paper—
And how a sad affair was mended
And Baby Darling's sorrow ended.

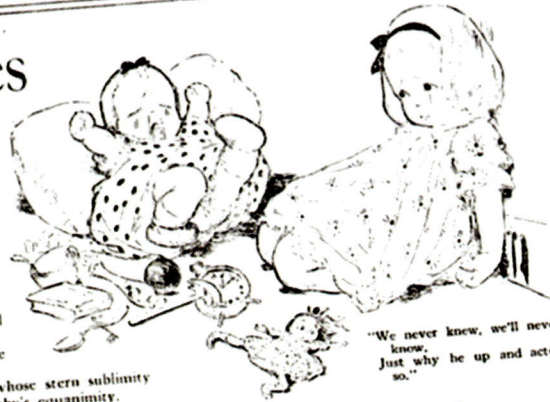

WELL, children dear, both far and near,
Again the Kewps are Kewping here!
Again those Kewpie wights are seen
Disporting in this magazine.
This magazine of note, I'm sure,
For sound and solid literature,
For serious thought and piety,
For wisdom and sobriety.

'Twould be more serious, no doubt of it,
If we could keep the Kewpies out of it;
But, dear me, when they once get in, you know,
The little duffers stick like sin, you know!

"That baby went on firmly howling,
At peper Kewpies simply scowling."

They've such a kind of, sort of way, you see,
We're, oh, so apt to stop and play, you see!
We let ourselves get fond (we did) of them,
And 'tis the mischief to get rid of them!
(We really don't know what to do about it!)

I fear we'll simply have to scan
This page as quickly as we can,
Cut out the dolls (and have *some* fun with it)
Then finish briskly and get done with it,
Thus leaving all our minds at leisure
For more improving work and pleasure:
For verbs, political economy,
Spelling, fractions, and astronomy.
At least, that is the way *I* do with it,
I Kewp a while, and then get through with it.

Now, when I mentioned "cutting out,"
It jogged my memory about;
In one way, or another, maybe,
Reminded of Dot Darling's baby.
(And here's the story:)

Well, I have told some other day
Of how Dot's family had a way
Of leaving Dot, so sweet and mild,
At home alone, to mind that child.
And, as a rule, dear
Dot enjoyed it;
At least, she never
did avoid it;
In fact, she rather
liked her luck,
you know;
The baby really was
a duck, you know,
Behaving with
a gay pro-
priety,
So one quite
relished his
society.
(He really was the
goodest kind
of a baby!)

But oh, 'tis dreadful
to relate
How fearful are the
ways of Fate!
For Fate it was whose stern sublimity
O'erthrew that baby's equanimity.
We'll never know, we never knew,
Why he should take the darker view;
Why he should take the darker view;
Why, suddenly, all life was cloud, you know,
And he should howl so very loud, you know.

We never knew, we'll never know,
Just why he up and acted so,
Just why he stamped
upon his doll
And broke his moth-
er's parasol,
And gave poor Dotty
such a knock,
And hammered so
upon the clock.

The way he threw
things left and
right
Was more or less
like dynamite,
He kicked each
thing Dot brought
to him,
Wild engines were
as naught to him.

He made one think
of desperadoes,
Volcanoes, tigers,
and tornadoes!

And how he roared! It sounded so!
No small child e'er resounded so!
The slowest neighbors took to scooting,
More active ones considered shooting.
(Oh, it was simply dreadful!)

Poor Dot could hardly speak, indeed,
She really felt quite weak indeed,
She tried to think of things to do,
She got the paste, and scizzors too.
"I'll cut some Kewpie dolls for you."
(Of course that *was* an idea!)

"We never knew, we'll never know,
Just why he up and acted so."

She cut out paper Kewps until
She had a lovely row, and still
That baby went on firmly howling,
At paper Kewpies simply scowling.
(But then something extraordinary
happened—)

Real Kewpies happened by that day!
And when poor Dot was turned away,
Hopped in, and with a sudden swoop
Removed each little paper Kewp;
And when Dot Darling turned her head,
Real Kewps were standing there instead!

Oh, dear, the change in Babe's expression!
He certainly lost all depression,
He surely lost all indication
Of recent mental perturbation.
Such joy was, maybe, never seen!
The happiest baby ever seen!

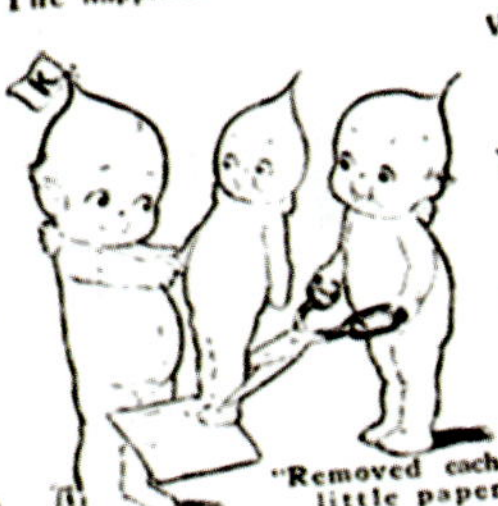

"Removed each little paper Kewp"

Well, dears,
when you
are cutting
out
Your Kewpie
dolls (well
cut, no
doubt),
I hope real
Kewps will
be about;
I hope when
paper
Kewps
you face,
dears,
Real Kewps may be there in their place, dears.
On this, I know, you can rely;
They will, if they *should* happen by.
If not, perhaps it's just as well, you know;
But look, for you can never tell, you know.

"Such joy was, maybe, never seen!
The happiest baby ever seen!"

October 1912.

The First of the Kewpie Kutouts

Presenting Wag, the Kewpie Chief; Dotty Darling, and Dotty Darling's Baby Brother

Designed and Painted by Rose O'Neill

(See Story—The Paper Kewpies—on Opposite Page)

Dotty Darling's Baby Brother—front view

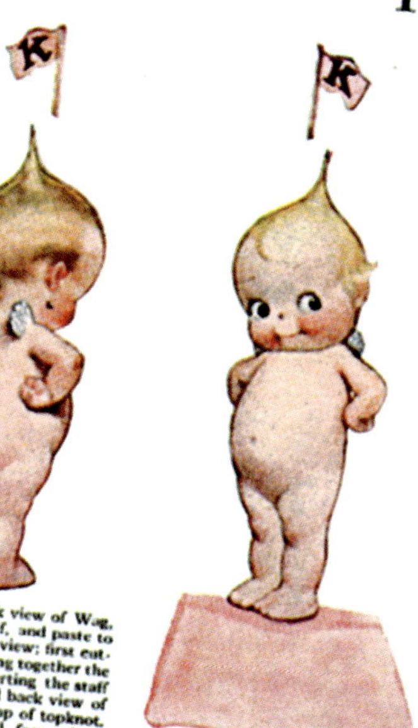

Cut out this back view of Wag, the Kewpie Chief, and paste to the cut-out front view; first cutting out and pasting together the little flag and inserting the staff between front and back view of Wag, just at the top of topknot. Bend red pedestal forward, so Wag will stand up by himself

Wag, the Kewpie Chief

This back view of Dotty Darling's Baby Brother is to be cut out and pasted to the front view. The little dress at the lower right-hand corner of the page is to be carefully cut out, then cut down the center of the back as far as the buttons go, and finally slipped over Baby Brother's head, so that the dress hangs on his shoulders

Cut out this back view of Dotty Darling, and paste on the back of the front view. Then cut out carefully Dotty Darling's every-day dress, and cut it down the back as far as the buttons go, so that you can slip the dress over Dotty's head and let it rest on her shoulders. After this, secure by folding back the tabs

Dotty Darling stands alone if you bend the red pedestal forward

Dotty Darling's Every-Day Dress

THERE will be more Kewpie Kutouts in coming issues of the COMPANION. Other members of Dotty Darling's family and others of the Kewpie Band will appear on the Kewpie Kutout page. Cut out the front and back of each figure, and paste together neatly, using as little paste as possible. Bend the entire pedestals forward at right angles to the figures, and the figures will stand alone

Baby Brother's Dress

November 1912.

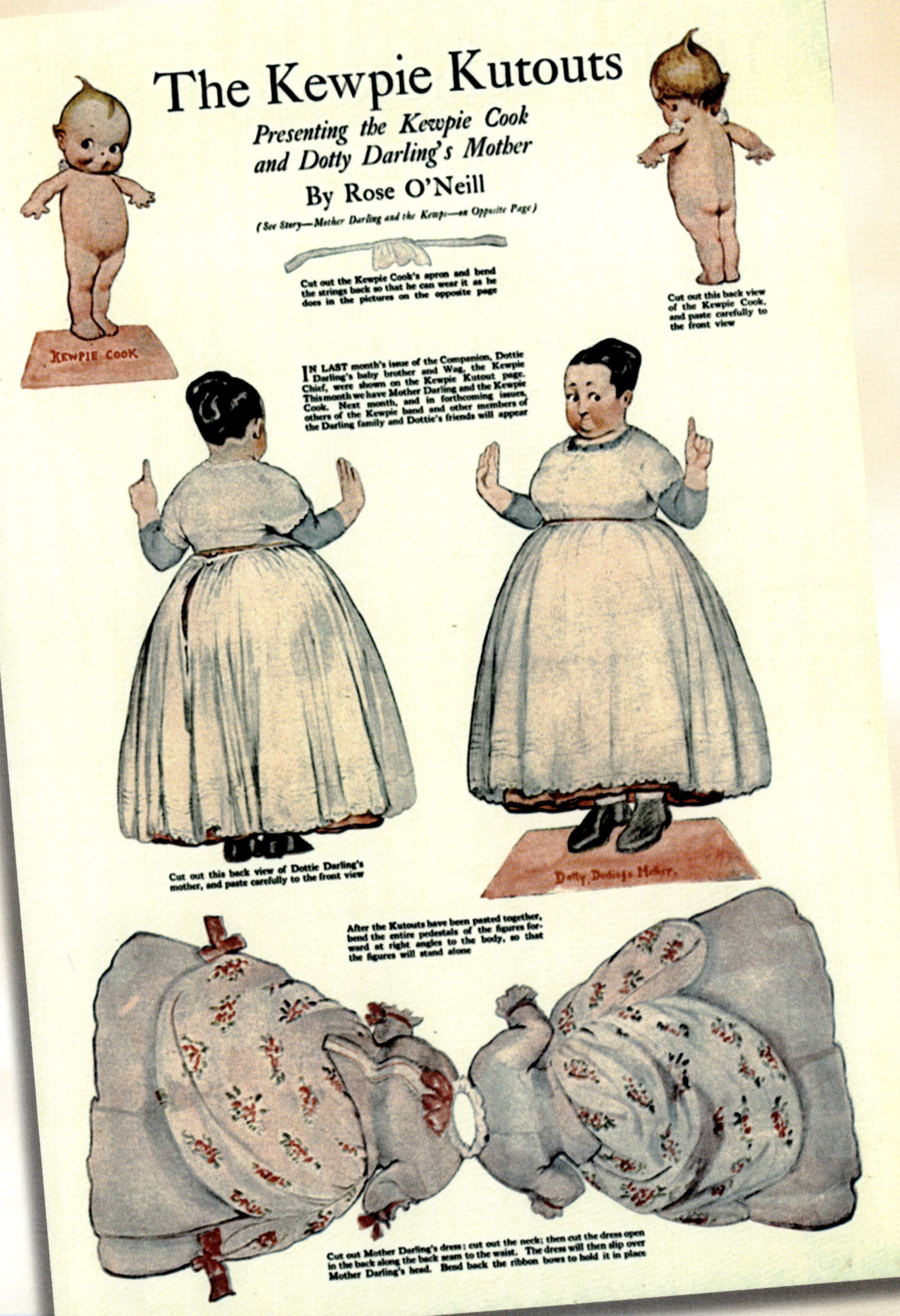

The Kewpie Kutouts

Presenting the Kewpie Cook and Dotty Darling's Mother

By Rose O'Neill

(See Story—Mother Darling and the Kewps—on Opposite Page)

Cut out the Kewpie Cook's apron and bend the strings back so that he can wear it as he does in the pictures on the opposite page

Cut out this back view of the Kewpie Cook, and paste carefully to the front view

KEWPIE COOK

IN LAST month's issue of the Companion, Dottie Darling's baby brother and Wag, the Kewpie Chief, were shown on the Kewpie Kutout page. This month we have Mother Darling and the Kewpie Cook. Next month, and in forthcoming issues, others of the Kewpie band and other members of the Darling family and Dottie's friends will appear

Cut out this back view of Dottie Darling's mother, and paste carefully to the front view

After the Kutouts have been pasted together, bend the entire pedestals of the figures forward at right angles to the body, so that the figures will stand alone

Cut out Mother Darling's dress; cut out the neck; then cut the dress open in the back along the back seam to the waist. The dress will then slip over Mother Darling's head. Bend back the ribbon bows to hold it in place

Stern Irene and the Kewpie Gardener

Third in the Series of Kewpie Kutouts

*(See Story—*The Kewps and Stern Irene*—on Opposite Page)*

This back view of the Kewpie Gardener is to be cut out and pasted carefully to the front view

THIS is the third of the Kewpie Kutouts that have come in the COMPANION to play with all the little girls and boys who know Dotty Darling and her adventures with the frolicsome Kewpies. In the October COMPANION were Dotty Darling herself and Baby Brother Darling, and their inseparable friend and companion, Wag the Chief. The Kewpie Cook (apron and all), accompanied by Mother Darling, appeared in the November issue. Now here are Irene Darling and the Kewpie Gardener. Other members of the Darling family and others of the Kewpie band will appear on this page in future issues of the COMPANION—a brand-new jolly set of playmates who are always ready to play all sorts of fascinating and entertaining Kewpish games

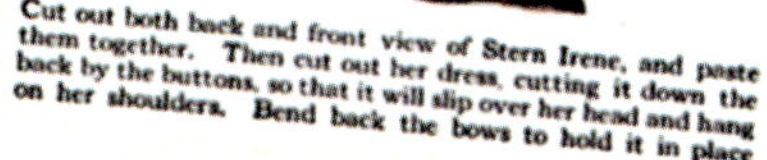
Cut out both back and front view of Stern Irene, and paste them together. Then cut out her dress, cutting it down the back by the buttons, so that it will slip over her head and hang on her shoulders. Bend back the bows to hold it in place

THE Kewpie Gardener, who appears on this page, is one of the most industrious of the Kewpie band. He finds so much work to do that he would get all worn out if he weren't a Kewpie. He takes his little rake and busies himself raking up the untidy paper-cuttings the children leave on the table when cutting out the Kewpie Kutouts. That reminds me, you must cut out the Gardener's rake and paste it in his little hand to help him to keep on with his work as a good Kewpie should

THE Kewpie Kutouts differ from all the other sorts of paper dolls because they have both back and front view. Cut out both views as carefully as you can, and paste them together, putting a light weight on them for a few minutes, so that they dry flat and even. Then bend the red base forward, so that the figure will stand upright. Cut out the dress all around, then cut out the neck, and slit the dress down the back along the buttons, so that it will slip easily over the head of the Kutout figure

MORE KEWPIE KUTOUTS COMING NEXT MONTH

January 1913.

The Kewpie Kutouts

Presenting the One that's Careful of his Voice and Dotty Darling's Sister Nan

By Rose O'Neill

(See Story—The Kewpies and Sister Nan—on Page 15)

Cut out this back view of the One that's Careful of his Voice, and paste it very carefully and neatly to this Kewp's front view

CHILDREN, LISTEN!

Eleven Kewpie Kutouts have already appeared in the Woman's Home Companion. Your Doll Family is not complete without them. You can get them all if you will turn to page 50 and act promptly

Cut out both back and front views of Sister Nan, and paste them together. Then put a light weight on her for a few minutes. After that, bend the red standard with her name on it so that she can stand upright. Slip her dress over her head and bend the sleeve-bows back to hold the dress in place at the wrist

This is Sister Nan's red-and-white plaid dress which is shown at the right. Cut it out neatly all around the edge, then cut out the neck very carefully, and be sure to slit it down the back where the buttons are. This makes it slip easily over Sister Nan's yellow hair. After it is on, bend the red ribbon bows back at the wrists to hold it properly and trimly in its place

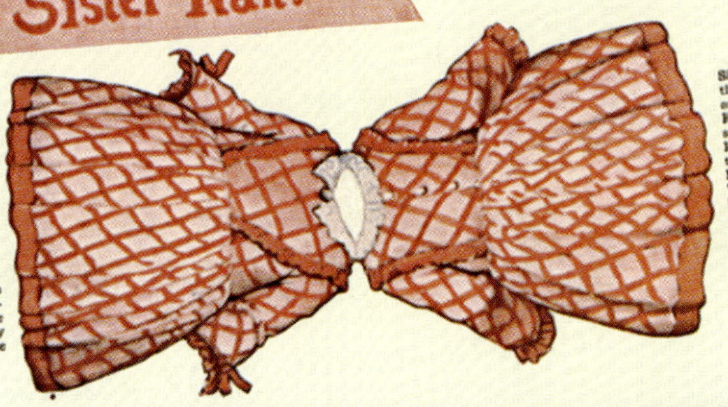

Sister Nan and the Kewp that's Careful of his Voice are the fourth in the set of Kewpie Kutouts to get themselves printed in the Woman's Home Companion. In October came Dotty Darling, Baby Brother Darling, and Wag the Chief; in November Mother Darling and the Kewpie Cook were seen, and in the December issue, Stern Irene and the Kewpie Gardener put in their appearance. Other Kewpies and Darlings will come later

The Kewpie Kutouts

Presenting the One Who Always Wears His Overshoes and Dotty Darling's Brother Dan

By Rose O'Neill

(*See Story*—The Kewpies and Brother Dan—on *Page 11*)

Cut out both the back and the front view of the Kewp Who Wears His Overshoes and paste the two views very neatly together. Put a light weight on them for a few minutes to keep them flat and even. Then bend the red base forward for the Kewp to stand up straight on

Cut out both the back and the front view of Brother Dan and paste them carefully together. Then bend the red base forward, so that Brother Dan can stand up

THIS is Brother Dan's little blue checked coat at the right. See the five bright brass buttons! Cut out the coat just as carefully as you can, and be sure to slit it up the front along the line of the brass buttons, and cut out the neck. Now slip the coat on Brother Dan right over his blue-and-white shirt with a square pink patch on the left elbow, and then bend back each cuff with the brass button on the flap. How Brother Dan hates to have his brand-new red suspenders all covered up!

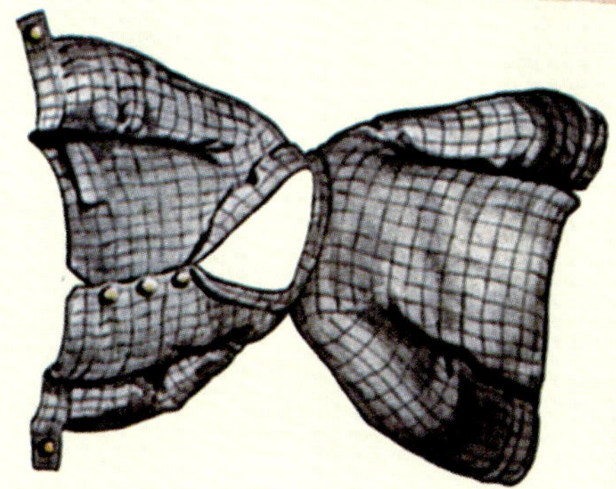

DOTTY DARLING, Baby Brother Darling, Mother Darling, Stern Irene Darling, Sister Nan, and now Brother Dan Darling have all come alive in the Kewpie Kutout series, and so have Wag the Chief, the Kewpie Cook, the Kewpie Gardener, the One That's Careful of His Voice, and the One That Wears His Overshoes.

In October, Dot and Baby Brother began to be paper doll folks; every month since then a Darling and a Kewp have come to play with you. Who do you suppose is next?

March 1913.

The Kewpie Kutouts

The Kewpie Army and The Orphan Boy

By Rose O'Neill

DO YOU ever feel cross? If you do, that is just the time to get out all your little Kewpie Kutout playmates with their jolly tricks and smiles. If Wag can't cheer you up, maybe the Cook can; and if the Cook can't, maybe the Gardener or the One That's Careful of His Voice or Always Wears His Overshoes can.

And then there's the whole Darling family ready to amuse you: the famous Dotty and her cunning Baby Brother, good Mother Darling, Sister Nan, Brother Dan and the Stern Irene. All these paper doll persons of the Kewpie Band and the Darling Household have been popping up two or three at a time in the Woman's Home Companion since October, 1912. Next month come more yet

Cut out this back view of the Kewpie Army, paste it neatly to the front view and bend the standard out straight. Be especially careful of the sword

To All Kewpie Lovers—Little and Large

Look on the "Dear Editor" page of this number and read the letters there that tell about some new ways Companion mothers and big sisters have found to make the Kewpie Kutouts wear better and last longer

LEFT, right! Left, right! Left right! The Kewpie Army comes marching into the Kutout page. Of course he wears a brave soldier's cap, and a leather sword-belt, and a bright little sword at his side, to say nothing of a very, very military air. The Kewpie Army is supposed to fight crossness, and crying, and whining, and all those other uncomfortable, not very cheerful things that little boys and girls sometimes like to do. Oh, how brave the Kewpie Army is!—not to be afraid of pouts and frowns and tears and such things. But then, you see, he has such cheerful little friends as Wag the Chief, and the Kewpie Cook, and the merry Gardener to play with all the time

THIS is the Orphan Boy who stands so forlornly at the right. You must cut him out carefully, and be sure not to shave his hair too closely, or he won't look sad and gloomy as he is supposed to look. When he is all cut out and his name-plate bent up to stand on, cut out the pail beside him, paying particular attention to the handle, which is hardest to cut

THE Kewpie Kutouts are not like any other magazine paper dolls in the world, for they are the only ones that have backs and fronts both. A very good plan after you have cut out their backs and fronts carefully and pasted them together is to place them under a light weight. This makes the back and front stick together neatly and keeps them flat. Don't put on too much paste either

Now you see the back of the Orphan Boy, and even his shabby elbows: one has a patch and the other has a hole. Cut out this back view of boy and pail, and paste to the front view. Stick the pail-handle in the right-hand doubled-up fist of the Orphan Boy

March 1913.

Page 79

The Kewpies and the Orphan Boy

Verses and Pictures by Rose O'Neill

(See the Kewpie Kutouts on Page 80)

HERE Kewpies teach us to be kind to
Even persons we've no mind to—
Hardly feel at all inclined to;
To duffers quite as well as dear ones,
To ragged, draggled little drear ones,
And sprawling, spindle-legged queer ones.

Now dears, when I get really going
With Kewpish rhymes, there is no knowing
Just when they will be dropping me;
There really is no stopping me.
One rhyme leads to another, so
I never know how far I'll go,
And ere I know what I'm about
I'm galloping like all get-out;
And find what is surprising, too,
I'm quite *enjoying* it, like you.
At least, I'm sure I hope you do.
If not, this page of Kewps, progressing,
Must be most painfully depressing,
The more so if you *have* to read, too.
(But maybe, you don't really need to.)

This month the subject of my pen—
The Darling family again!
Now, as you know, the family had
Three daughters and a little lad,
A baby too; there was, of course,
Considerable work, perforce.
So much a home like that requires,
Chopping wood and lighting fires;
The very dickens, shoveling, weeding,
Ducks and chickens needing feeding.
And so they had, for out-of-doors,
An orphan boy to do the chores,
And I regret to say, my dears,
That boy was oft reduced to tears.
The children of that family
Were *not* as kind as they should be.
(Excepting Dot.) It was their joy
To tease that timid orphan boy.
The orphan, standing sadly by,
Would lift to them his mild, blue eye,
As if he mutely would entreat
Them not to tread on him complete—
Upon his feelings and his feet.
(Poor little fellow!)

This only seemed to stimulate
Their tendency to agitate;
They mocked his manner apprehensive,
And his expression somewhat pensive;
Mocked his walking in the road, too,
And his standing pigeon-toed, too,
And the cut of his suspender,
Mentioning in words un-tender
That his legs were rather slender.
"Shamble-jambed," I think they called him,
With other things that quite appalled him,
And then they instigated Towser
To tear his ragged little trouser.
(Things *couldn't* be worse.)

The children of that family
Were not as kind as they should be

When some wild geese went flopping there
And from their backs came dropping there
The Kewpies lightly hopping there.
Said Wag, "I've often noted here
The way you treat this orphan dear,
Now, goodness knows how they will serve us.
And just to teach you how 'twould be,
You shall be orphans, all you three.
We'll take you off for many a mile
And you'll be orphans for a while."
Then, through the air the three careen,
Young Nan and Dan and Stern Irene,
To where there dwells a dame severe,
A vigorous mind with views austere
Said Wag: "Miss Grimes, here at your doors
Are orphans three to do your chores."
Said she, "Oh, Law! I'm quite surprised,
I wish I'd never advertised!
An orphan *always* makes me nervous!
But, Lawk! Don't stare there any more!
If you *have* come to chore, why *chore!*"
(So the Kewpies left them there.)

She said, "Oh, Law! I'm quite surprised,
I wish I'd never advertised!"

And now, I can lay down the pen, my dears,
For when those three came home again, my dears,
Kind deeds became their hourly joy, you see,
Conferred upon their orphan boy, you see:
"For we've been orphans," little Nan explained,
"And we've done chores," young thoughtful Dan explained,
And as for Stern Irene, her smile, they say,
Was strangely meek for quite a while, they say.

And for the orphan boy, by scores
The Kewpies helped him with his chores,
No longer tiresome and tearful,
They taught him to be bright and cheerful.

And for the orphan boy, by scores
The Kewpies helped him with his chores

May 1913.

How the Kewps Turned into Dolls

Verses and Pictures by Rose O'Neill

'TIS nearly May! oh, dear, oh, *dear!*
The darling month of all the year!
The winter wanes on weary wing,
The world is comforted with spring.
Young flowers console the lonely places
With the sweetness of their faces.
The birds are coming, mile on mile,
Our northern sadness to beguile.
The trees all nurse their buds and smile.
They nurse their buds and cling to them,
And talk of splendid spring to them,
Of lovely leaves they sing to them.
They rock their buds on every breeze,

"Why, certainly," said Wag, and smiled.
"There's Kewps enough for every child.
There's Kewps enough by tens and dozens
For all the children and their cousins.
In Kewpie Land, that paradise,
They're *always* making fresh supplies."
(Which is quite true, you know.)

"He gives you information on the spot"

He falls off walls, or trees, or mountains, maybe,
Because he's bent on being like a baby.
At stubbing toes, he is a wonder too.
(See one tied up.) We call him Blunderboo.

"And now, dear Dot, that's all I'll name to-day;
Let's talk, instead, of why we came to-day.
As o'er your roof we Kewps were swishing now,
We heard our Dot engaged in wishing, now.
And down we dropped.
So, dear, proceed to mention

Oh, what a lark!" the Kewpies cried.
(Great excitement!)

"*Poor* children first," cried Dotty Darling,
And off each Kewp flew like a starling.
They carried boxes for a week or two,
And sometimes there would be a squeak or two
(They'd hear it, though the Kewps were chaffing so)
From inside, where the "doll" was laughing so.
And children—when those dolls came to them!
Thrills of rapture went right through them!
"Oh, look!" they'd cry. "Oh, look at this one!
Oh, let me, let me, let me kiss one!"
(Those Kewps made the *best* behaved dolls!)

"Quick, run and get the rest of us. Put doll clothes on the best of us"

Those blissful, kissful, mother trees.
They lull their buds with melodies.
And while they're gently holding them
(No hurrying or scolding them),
They're softly—*soft*—unfolding them.
(Oh, sweet mother trees!)

"And now," said Dotty Darling mild,
"With happiness I'm nearly wild.
I wish that every single child
Could have a Kewpie for its own,
To stay with it and play with it
And just *belong* to it alone.
If it *could* be—for every tree
Has its *own* buds: that's plain to see.
And if the Kewpies really could
Arrange it so, I wish they would,—
Beginning, please, with Babe and me,—
That's if they *might*, conveniently."
(And what do you suppose—?)

No sooner had she finished speaking
Than she heard the door a-creaking,
And there was all the Kewpie band
With thousands more from Kewpie Land.
"Dear me!" said Dotty, are there *more?*
Such crowds I never saw before!"

"Dear me!" said Dot, "look, here are two loves
That look to me distinctly new loves!"
"Permit me, I shall introduce a few."
Said Wag, "Of course we'll have to lose a few.
In such a crowd you can't get *all* the names;
You simply can't, somehow, recall the names.
But here's the first, the wisest of the lot,
He gives you information on the spot.
All points he settles with a look, you know,
At his extraordinary book, you know.
On trips, Instructive Kewps are good, besides
For finding Lat. and Longitude, besides.
The next new Kewpie offered for inspection
With a sunbonnet cares for his complexion.
The next wears life preservers, quick to clap on,
As one can never tell just *what* may happen.
This little chap has really great renown:
The only Kewp that's always falling down.

Your wish, assured you have our rapt attention."
(Thus Wag finished his rather long speech.)

"I *did* wish something, with a great big W.
But, really, I am so afraid 'twould trouble you,"
So Dot rejoined, grown rather shy, at once.
But all the Kewpies make reply at once,
And look particularly spry, at once.
So Dot takes courage, and says, modestly,
"I wished that you'd turn into dolls, you see,
So every single childie could have one
To stay with it and play with it."
The Kewps replied, "No sooner said than done.
'Twill be the most resplendent bit of fun!
Quick, run and get the rest of us.
Put doll clothes on the best of us.
Bring boxes now and get inside.
With ribbons every box be tied!

"We'll turn back into Kewps again"

And Dot and Baby Brother, too,
Kissed theirs enough to smother two,
"If children should be *bad*, of course,
Unkind and cross and mad, of course,"
The Kewpie dolls said, "then, with pain,
We'll turn back into Kewps again,
And off we'll fly in little flocks
And leave them just an empty box.
But, thanks to goodness, children bad
Are *very* seldom to be had.
At least, 'tis sure there aren't many;
In fact, we don't believe there's *any*."
(And I *do* hope they were right!)

They carried boxes for a week or two

May 1913.

Page 22 WOMAN'S HOME COMPANION

May, 1913

The Flying Kewpies

A New and Fascinating Kewpish Family

By Rose O'Neill

(To find out all about them, read the verses on page 15)

The Life Preserver Kewpie

CUT out the life belt you see at the right and paste it neatly and firmly around the middle of this Kewpie. He always wears a life preserver buckled around his waist when flying—as he says, you never can tell *what* may happen

The Kewpie Life Preserver

TO MAKE the Flying Kewpies, first cut out both back and front views carefully. Just before you paste the back and front together, place the end of a string between the front and the back of the head. Put a slight weight on the Kewpie to keep him flat, and when he is dry you can hang him up by his string from the chandelier, and play he is flying

Back of Life Preserver Kewpie

NO WONDER this Kewpie wears a life preserver. Probably he thinks that the little boy or girl who pastes the string into his head won't use enough glue. What would happen then? An awful tumble! He might even have to be tied up like Blunderboo

Careful of his Complexion

CAREFUL of his Complexion, you see, wears a sunbonnet tied under his chin. This protects his face from the breeze when he is flying fast, and shades his eyes from sunshine and lamplight. Watch how gaily the strings and ruffle flutter when he flies

Blunderboo, the Kewpie that is always tumbling

Back of Careful of his Complexion

JUST suppose Careful of his Complexion should get freckles! Or tan his nose! A dreadful thought! So he wears a sunbonnet, which he knows looks very cunning. No doubt he has a jar of cold cream somewhere to use after long flying trips

Back of Blunderboo

BLUNDERBOO, the Kewpie that is always tumbling, wears one toe tied up because he likes to pretend that he has stubbed it, like a real baby. If Blunderboo had *really* stubbed his toe he would not be looking so cheerful

Instructive Kewpie

CUT out the back and front of Instructive Kewpie's big book at the right and paste them together. Then press Instructive Kewpie's arms forward to clasp it against his breast. His eyes may *just* peep out over the edge of the book. How wise Instructive Kewpie looks! He has studied so much that he knows his book by heart

Back of Instructive Kewpie

INSTRUCTIVE Kewpie can fly as far and fast as any of the other Flying Kewpies, in spite of his fat book. The print in the "Compendium of Useful Knowledge" is so fine that Instructive Kewpie has to wear large glasses with horn rims, like a real teacher. You see, he almost ruined his eyesight once, reading while flying

June 1913.

The Kewpie Kutouts

Little Assunta and Her Kewpie Doll

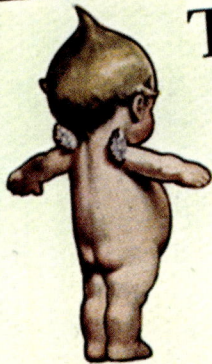

By Rose O'Neill

Children, look on page 15 if you want to read the story of Little Assunta and the Kewpie Doll

This is the back of Kewpie Doll. Cut it out and paste to the cut-out front of Kewpie Doll. Bend up standard, and he is done

Cut out Kewpie Doll's little flower dress and slit it down the line of buttons in the back

NOTICE Kewpie Doll's dress. It is, you see, sprinkled with little red daisies and tied with four red ribbons to match. Kewpie Doll wears a flower dress because it is June and there are flowers growing everywhere, except in city streets. Kewpie Doll knows of yellow buttercups in fields and pink roses in gardens. Perhaps Kewpie Doll thinks that flowers in a dress are better than no flowers at all for Little Assunta, who lives in the slums. When you have slipped the dress over Kewpie Doll's little peaked topknot and wings, be sure to bend back the ribbon bows on the sleeves and on the skirt to hold it neatly

THE red dress is Little Assunta's best one. It is just the color of her father's working shirt and her mother's big silk handkerchief, which she ties over her head when she goes on the street. There are at least five holes in Little Assunta's best dress, and the very biggest one has not been mended yet. Maybe Little Assunta's mother had no more patches, or maybe she is so busy taking care of Little Assunta's brothers and sisters that she doesn't have time to sew. Very likely when Little Assunta sees how clean and neat Kewpie Doll's dress is, she will beg her mother to mend the hole, even if the patch has to be purple, or pink, or green, or yellow

Cut out around the ragged edges of Assunta's red dress, and slit down the line of buttons

LITTLE ASSUNTA

THIS is sad Little Assunta before Kewpie Doll found her sitting forlornly beside the garbage barrel. She is very, very poor, and wears a ragged dress and shoes that are out at the toes. She has no nice place to play, like little country children—only dark, dirty streets, instead of picnic woods and hayfields. Little Assunta hasn't even a dolly—or she didn't have till Kewpie Doll came flying along. How her black eyes sparkled when she saw Kewpie Doll and hugged him tight!

THIS is the back view of Little Assunta. Cut it out carefully and paste to the front view. Then lay Little Assunta under a light weight so that she will be smooth and flat. Bend up the red name plate, and let her stand by herself.

Little Assunta has on her every-day dress which, you see, she once tore terribly on a nail sticking out from an old egg crate. Her red dress, too, has had hard wear. When you cut it out be careful not to jab any more holes in it with your scissors. Slip it gently over Little Assunta's head and bend the ribbons back to hold it on. You cannot possibly be as poor and sad as Little Assunta, but maybe the Kewpie doll will make you happy sometimes

July 1913.

Page 28 WOMAN'S HOME COMPANION July, 1913

Dotty and Four of Her Kewpie Friends

By Rose O'Neill

Kewpie Gardener

Cut out the front and back view of each Kewpie and paste the front view carefully to the back view. Lay the Kewpie under a weight while the paste is drying. Bend the red pedestal forward so that the Kewpie can stand by himself. Be sure to paste Wag's flag and Kewpie Gardener's rake right where they belong

Wag, the Kewpie Chief

Back of Careful of His Voice

Careful of his Voice.

This back view of the Kewpie Gardener is to be cut out and pasted carefully to the front view

Cut out the Kewpie Cook's apron and bend the strings back so that he can wear it as he does in the pictures on the preceding page

KEWPIE COOK

Dotty Darling's Everyday Dress

Cut out this back view of Dotty Darling and paste on the back of the front view. Then cut out carefully Dotty Darling's everyday dress, and cut it down the back as far as the buttons go, so that you can slip the dress over Dotty's head and let it rest on her shoulders. After this, secure by folding back the tabs

Dotty Darling stands alone if you bend the red pedestal forward

DOTTY DARLING and her best Kewpie friends were so popular when they first appeared that the magazines containing them were sold out before all the little boys and girls who wanted them could get Dotty and Wag and Kewpie Gardener and Kewpie Cook and Careful of His Voice. That is why they are printed again on this page—now you can have a Dotty and Kewpie series complete

Back of Kewpie Cook, to be cut out and pasted to front

The Kewpies and Little Samuel

Verses and Pictures by Rose O'Neill

Well, if you could have seen the knack! They up and paint one Kewpie black

In this old barrel he would squeeze, And sit there like Diogenes

THIS month the tale I have to tell
Relates to little Samuel,
To Samuel de Vere Leroy,
A pleasant little colored boy,
He had some sorrows in his lot;
A single playmate he had not.
His neighbors all were white, you know,
And did not think it right, you know,
To share their joys or toys at all,
Or play with colored boys at all.

His mother had a painful way
Of arguing the lifelong day.
Her favorite topics were religions,
Etiquette, and carrier pigeons,
The price of prunes, the Presidents,
And if the moon has residents;
She'd speak of tonics and temptations,
Of laws, and laundries, and relations,
Of soap and sinful recreations.
She spoke with free gesticulations.
She spoke with vigor, did the mammy
Of poor unhappy little Sammy.
And when her son was fain to fly,
She held him with her glittering eye.
Poor Sammy tried her words to cherish,
But, oh, he thought that he would perish!
Then, when he did get out at last,
The children shouted, as they passed,
Threw teasing "names" in his direction,
And made remarks on his complexion.
(It really was *pretty* hard on him!)

In this old barrel he would squeeze,
And sit there like Diogenes;
And there the little Kewpies found him,
Hopped, and flopped, and fluttered 'round him.

"At first," said Wag, "some bread and jam,
And then a Kewpie doll for Sam!
Let's make it 'colored' if we can,
And dress it like this little man."
Well, if you could have seen the knack!
They up and paint one Kewpie black,
His tiny trousers shape with taste,
And button up his little waist.
Then, "Here's a Kewpie doll for you.
We hope you like it 'colored,' too."

And Sammy went, with soul unruffled, While Min McCoy behind him scuffled

Young Sammy *can't* believe it's true!
(Oh, that *happy* little boy!)

Well, dears, I simply lack the power
To tell of Sammy from that hour.
He seemed a different youngster, quite,
His Kewpie with him, day and night.
In situations fraught with pain
The Kewp would stimulate his brain;
When Min McCoy, a neighbor's child,
In purest Irish undefiled,
Poured forth such terms as drive one wild,
And, jumping up and down with vim,
Made awful faces straight at him,
The Kewpie said, "In such a case
I think *I'd* simply leave the place.
When circumstances jar, you know,
Perhaps the best thing is to *go*."
And Sammy *went*, with soul unruffled,
While Min McCoy behind him scuffled,
Her baby brother tumbling, flump!—
But saved by Kewpies from a bump.

And when his mother argued questions
That might disturb the best digestions
The dolly whispered, "Now, you know,
It would not be polite to *go*;
That treatment of this painful case
Would be a little out of place,
So I'd advise you just to smile
And think of something else a while.
When arguments your mind derange,
Why, give your mental powers a change,
Until a pause; then say, and bow,
'Excuse me, but I'm going now.'
Keep looking pleasant while you drop away.
Just make your little bow, and hop away."

And so, through Sammy's whole existence,
The Kewp, with mild but firm persistence,
Gave good advice to meet the urgency
Of each and every fresh emergency.
The kernel of his wisdom, see,
When matters go distressingly,
Is just to *GO*, as if on wings;
Or stay, and *THINK OF OTHER THINGS.*

The dolly whispered, "Now, you know It would not be polite to go

August 1913.

The Musical Kewpies
and the Little German Girl

By ROSE O'NEILL

(The full story of the Musical Kewpies is on page 35)

Cut out Katerina's little pinafore at the left, slit it down the line of four buttons in the back, and then bend up the flaps to hold it on firmly

TOOT—tooty—toot—*toot*—toot!
The Kewpies are coming to
town. Wag marches ahead of the
band, tum—tumty—tum—*tum*—
tum, and all the brisk little, gay
little, kind little Kewps step after.
They simply *glory* in pleasing Katerina by playing band music; and they
make the biggest kind of brass blare
they can. Life Preserver Kewpie
bears the big bass drum on his
back, Careful of His Voice beats
and bangs it loud and long, and
Always Wears His Overshoes says
they keep his toes *from* getting
tired when he marches. As for
Kewpie Army, he shoulders his gun
and plays he is going to the war

DID you ever get a Musical Present? Say a
drum, or a horn, or a mouth organ? No doubt!
But you never had one like Katerina's, a big brass
trumpet thing with a real Kewpie inside of it. To
make the Musical Present, cut out the back and
front of it very carefully, paste them together and
bend the red standard so the horn stands straight up

THESE famous Kewpie Kutouts! The
paper dolls with both backs and fronts!
Katerina, the little German girl, and Musical
Present are two more of them! To make
Katerina, cut out the back and front of her
most carefully, without slicing her fat cheeks
or shearing her braids, or paring off any of the
cloth in that puffy little skirt that Katerina's
mother made. Paste the back and front
together without using *too* much paste. Be
sure to place the back and front so that they
exactly fit. Lay Katerina under a slight
weight till the paste is dry. This keeps her
flat and smooth. Bend up the red standard,
and there Katerina is, beaming at you with
her round little blue eyes just as she beamed
at the Kewpie band when they came tootling
and piping past the windows of her house

LITTLE Katerina is *so* musical, and especially fond of
bands. When she saw the Kewpie band and heard
them play she just bounced up and down and round and
round. Even her seven petticoats didn't stop her, and her
smooth little yellow pigtails stood right out straight. She
was so thankful to the Kewpies for their beautiful band
music that she ran and asked her mother for a pretzel to
give to every one of them. Katerina has a warm little heart

The Wealthy Kewpie and the Wealthy Child

By Rose O'Neill

(The full story of these two will be found on page 15)

THE nicest Kutouts in the world are these, because every single little Kewpie and every single Kewpie friend has a back and a front. Even the poorest little Kewp has one back and one front, and Wealthy Kewpie has no more than one back and one front. To make the Kewpie Kutouts, your best plan is to cut out each back and each front separately very carefully, paste them together with a very little glue, and lay them under a light weight to keep them smooth and flat. When they are perfectly dry, bend up the standards.

Of course the dresses, when there are any, have backs and fronts too, and you always find ribbon bows to bend back and hold them on.

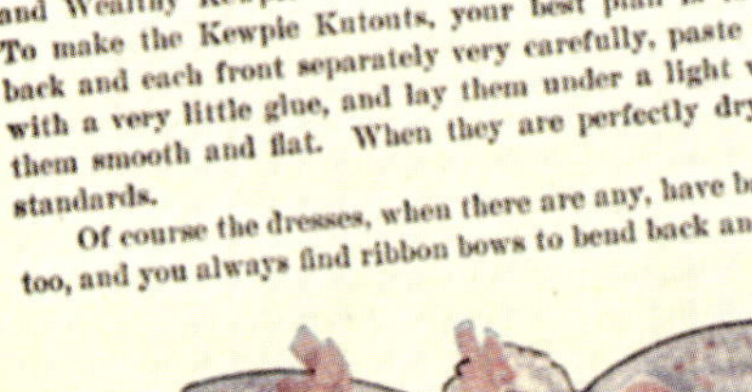

Wealthy Kewpie.

CUT out the front view of Wealthy Kewpie, paste it to the back view and bend up the red platform for him to stand on. Wealthy Kewpie, you see, looks quite like any other Kewpie until he puts on his frilly little dress

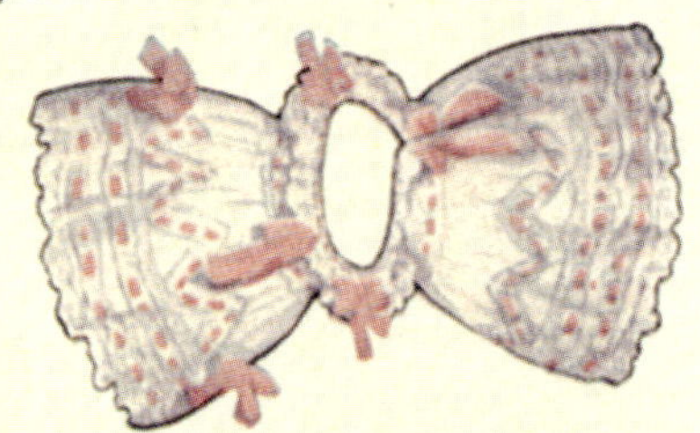

Cut out Wealthy Kewpie's little fancy frock, slit it between the two bows in the back and slide it over his head, bending over the bows to hold it on neatly

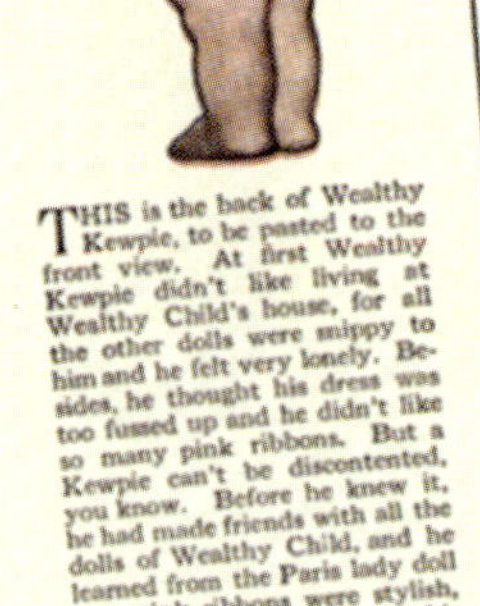

THIS is the back of Wealthy Kewpie, to be pasted to the front view. At first Wealthy Kewpie didn't like living at Wealthy Child's house, for all the other dolls were snippy to him and he felt very lonely. Besides, he thought his dress was too fussed up and he didn't like so many pink ribbons. But a Kewpie can't be discontented, you know. Before he knew it, he had made friends with all the dolls of Wealthy Child, and he learned from the Paris lady doll that pink ribbons were stylish, so he didn't mind wearing his new dress. He even admired it

Wealthy Child.

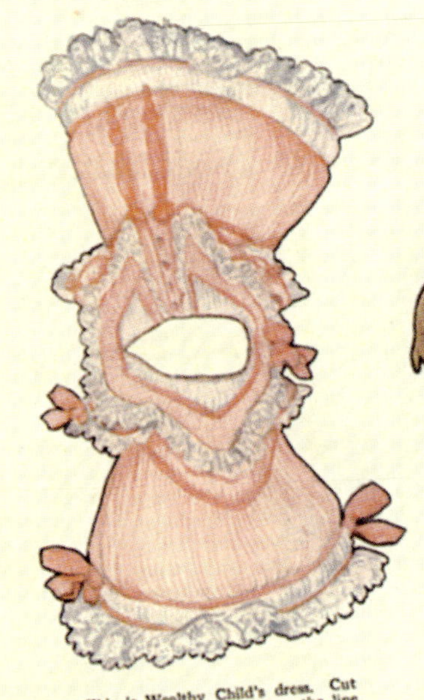

This is Wealthy Child's dress. Cut it out carefully, slit it down the line of buttons. Slip it over Wealthy Child's curls and bend back the bows

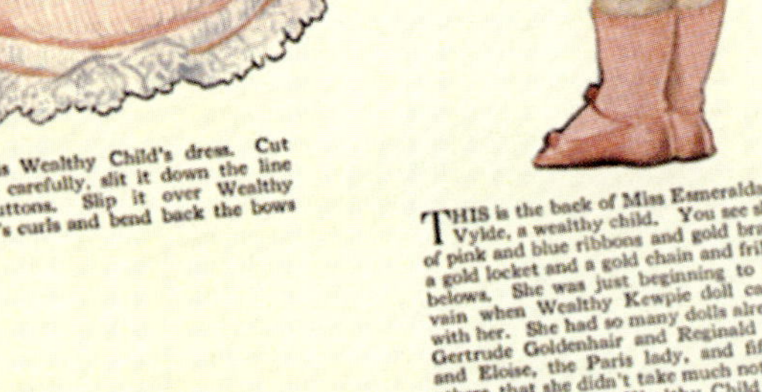

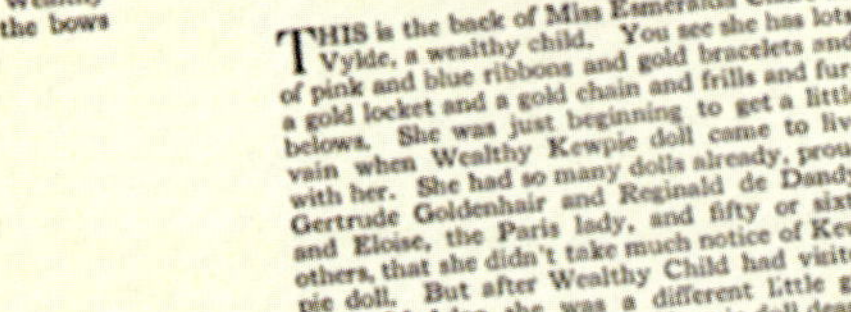

THIS is the back of Miss Esmeralda Claire de Vylde, a wealthy child. You see she has lots of pink and blue ribbons and gold bracelets and a gold locket and a gold chain and frills and furbelows. She was just beginning to get a little vain when Wealthy Kewpie doll came to live with her. She had so many dolls already, proud Gertrude Goldenhair and Reginald de Dandy, and Eloise, the Paris lady, and fifty or sixty others, that she didn't take much notice of Kewpie doll. But after Wealthy Child had visited Susan McAdoo she was a different little girl and couldn't help loving her Kewpie doll dearly

October 1913.

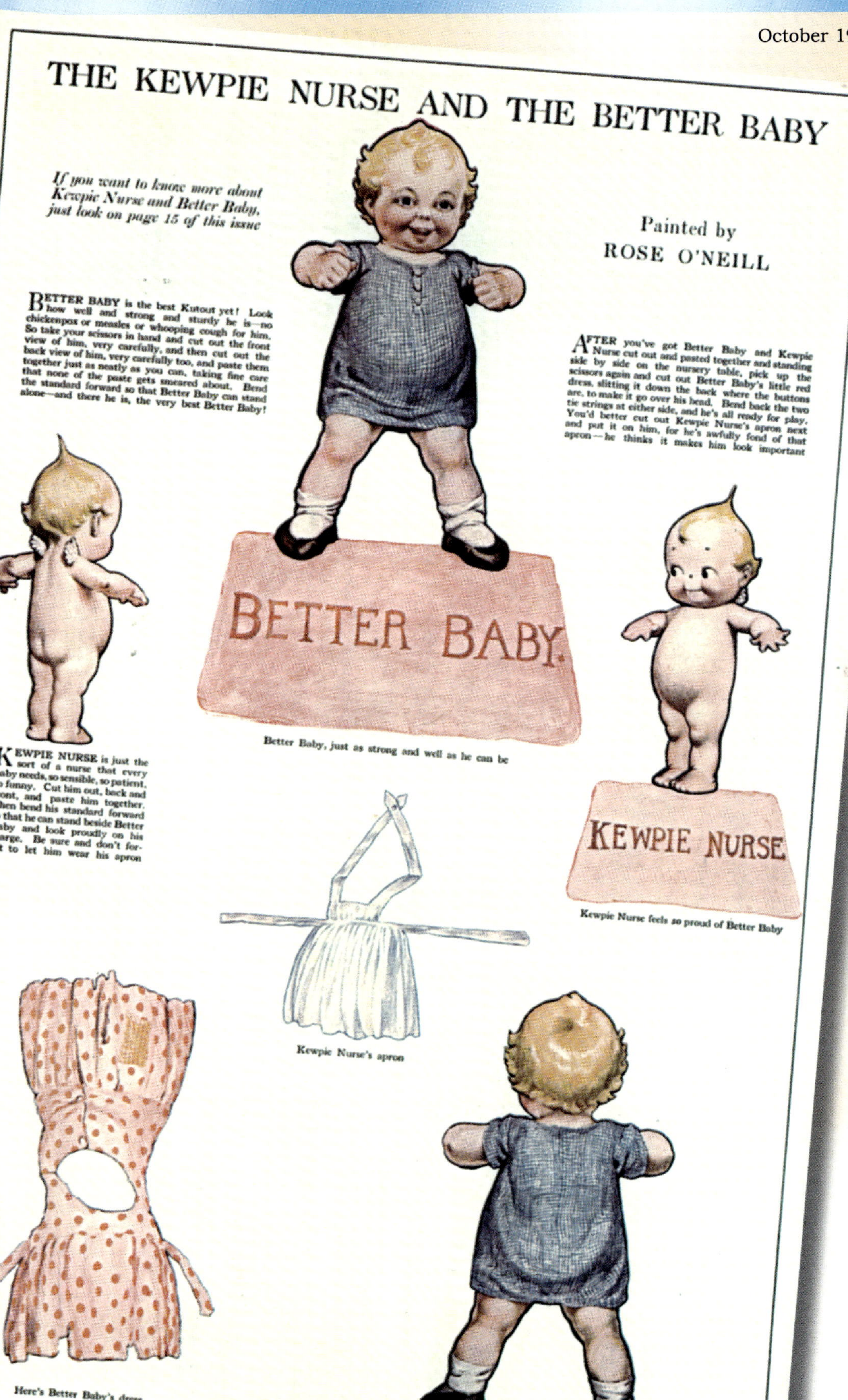

THE KEWPIE NURSE AND THE BETTER BABY

If you want to know more about Kewpie Nurse and Better Baby, just look on page 15 of this issue

Painted by
ROSE O'NEILL

BETTER BABY is the best Kutout yet! Look how well and strong and sturdy he is—no chickenpox or measles or whooping cough for him. So take your scissors in hand and cut out the front view of him, very carefully, and then cut out the back view of him, very carefully too, and paste them together just as neatly as you can, taking fine care that none of the paste gets smeared about. Bend the standard forward so that Better Baby can stand alone—and there he is, the very best Better Baby!

AFTER you've got Better Baby and Kewpie Nurse cut out and pasted together and standing side by side on the nursery table, pick up the scissors again and cut out Better Baby's little red dress, slitting it down the back where the buttons are, to make it go over his head. Bend back the two tie strings at either side, and he's all ready for play. You'd better cut out Kewpie Nurse's apron next and put it on him, for he's awfully fond of that apron—he thinks it makes him look important

Better Baby, just as strong and well as he can be

KEWPIE NURSE is just the sort of a nurse that every baby needs, so sensible, so patient, so funny. Cut him out, back and front, and paste him together. Then bend his standard forward so that he can stand beside Better Baby and look proudly on his charge. Be sure and don't forget to let him wear his apron

Kewpie Nurse feels so proud of Better Baby

Kewpie Nurse's apron

Here's Better Baby's dress

Cut out Better Baby's back and paste to his front

THE KEWPIE DOG AND THE BAD LITTLE BOY

BY ROSE O'NEILL

(Look on page 11 for the whole story)

THIS is the Kewpie who is playing he's naughty, like Bad Little Boy. Paste his cut-out back view to his cut-out front view, lay him under a weight and then bend him up so he can stand upon his platform winking away as hard as he can

Bad Little Bill Tibbs really thinks it is funny to tease and torture little dogs! Note his naughty wink

Front view of Kewpie Winking Like Bad Little Boy

LISTEN children! Why don't you give a real Kewpie present this Christmas? Any of the Kewpie Kutouts will delight your friends young and old. You can choose a Kutout, pack it in a little box or put it in a Christmas envelope and send it with your love the day before Christmas. Kewpies like to be Christmas presents.

Next year the Kewpies are going to hold parties on the Entertainment pages of the COMPANION. Some of the parties will be for little folks and some for grown-ups, but the very same Kewpies will be there. Just watch and see!

THE Kewpies love Christmas time because it gives them so many chances to cheer up people and play kind little tricks. Sometimes they go and hang themselves on Christmas tree branches among the popcorn chains and tinsel to please little girls and boys. Kewpie Winking Like Bad Little Boy is just doing it now to make a little girl stop crying. Kewpie Cook makes delicious Christmas goodies for little poor children like the Orphan Boy, and once the Kewpie that's Careful of His Voice sang Christmas carols to a lonesome old lady who couldn't spend Christmas with her grandchildren

LOOK out for the Kewps! When they begin to take you in hand you *have* to behave. And they are sure to treat you just the way you have been treating someone else. Bad Little Boy soon had enough of being chased and scared with rattling tin pans and pails tied all over him. He didn't tease any more dogs for many a day.

As for the little Doggie he became a great pet with the Kewpies. They all wanted to play with him; Wag taught him how to sit up straight like a soldier, Kewpie Cook made him some Kewpie Dog Biscuit and Kewpie Gardener told him he might bury bones in the garden if he wouldn't scratch the flower beds.

Kewpie Dog soon became very helpful to the Kewpies in teaching Bad Little Boys how not to treat dogs and cats

THREE more Kewpie Kutouts for you, Kewpie friends! And everyone has a back and a front. That makes them seem real, hardly like paper dolls at all. They are the only Kutouts in the world, you know, that have backs and fronts. The best of it is, the backs are just as amusing as the fronts, quite often. Look at Kewpie Dog's back or the back of Kewpie Winking Like Bad Little Boy!

Every back and front has to be cut out *so* carefully with your scissors and then the proper backs and fronts have to be stuck together with a little paste—not too much to be messy. After that you lay them under a slight weight until they are flat and smooth and dry. Then you may bend up the standards. Look next year for more Kewps in WOMAN'S HOME COMPANION

EVEN the back of Bad Little Bill Tibbs makes you pity the dogs and cats that come his way. Cut out this view, paste it to the front view and bend Bill at the waist line. This makes him seem to be sitting with his legs crossed just as he sat in a tenement doorstep to watch Kewpie Dog run down the street with the tomato can on his tail

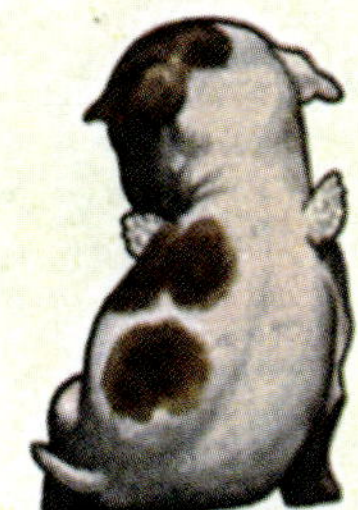

KEWPIE Dog flies around now, looking after all little forlorn, homeless doggies. You see, he remembers how *he* felt before the Kewps befriended him, and he knows he is needed whenever he sees a Bad Little Boy who acts like Bill Tibbs

How proud Kewpie Dog is of his new wings!

This is the tin tomato can that Bad Little Boy tied to Kewpie Dog's tail. Paste the front view to the back view

January 1914.

THE KEWPIES AND SANTA CLAUS

Verse and Pictures

BY ROSE O'NEILL

"I wonder if I'm getting old,
Or simply caught a bit of cold,"
Said Santa Claus one Christmas Eve.
"My joints are creaking, I believe,—
At least, when I began to speak,
I thought I heard a sort of squeak!"
He laughed, the gay old cockalorum,
As if he didn't *much* deplore 'em,
As if enjoying (while he spoke on)
A set of joints he had a joke on.
"And children! Why, a million score of 'em!
And every blessed year there's more of 'em!
All waiting for this plump old codger there
To find each house and little lodger there!
Quite easy for old Claus to ride, for them,
Through every town and countryside for them,
And down their chimneys lightly slide for them,
The little darlings think, and so, of course,
Old Claus must harness up and go, of course!

"And yet" (he winked with rosy glee, you know),
"I think I'd rather like to see, you know,
What sort of chap would try to rob
Me of my fine old Christmas job!
No creak or squeak would count a whit,
He'd have a lively time of it!
I'd brush his manners up a bit!"
His laughter woke the echoes distant.
"And yet," he said, "a spry assistant . . ."
"A spry assistant, did you say, sir?
Why here are dozens, brisk and gay, sir!"
Old Santa turned and, close at hand,
There stood the little Kewpie band!
(Well, you should have heard him shout!)

"Come, pack his dear old sleigh," cried Wag.
"Put Kewpie dolls in every bag.
Now harness up his reindeer swift
And give our darling saint a lift.
Climb in! We're off through purple distance!
Now, how is that for spry assistance!"
"Dear me," said Santa, 'mid the cheers,
"How *have* I got on all these years!
These Kewpies sure have points about 'em,
I don't see how I've done without 'em!"
Across the snow, o'er roofs they sped,
A million children visited
And stockings filled with speed surprising.
Said Santa, "This is paralyzing!
These Kewpies are most enterprising!"
(Oh, my, how fast they went!)

But soon Claus grumbled, "Looky there!
New-fangled chimneys I *can't* bear!
A chap like me can *not* get down 'em,
Though children's tears should simply drown 'em!
So many houses have that kind, of late,
My figure folks don't bear in mind, of late.
No fireplace, no chimneys wide, now,
No room for Santa Claus to slide, now!
What *will* become of Christmas-tide now!"

The reindeer pawed the snow about,
The Kewpies stood in thoughtful doubt;
The wind blew o'er the roof the sleet,
Old Santa danced to warm his feet.
The Kewps laughed at his coat of sable
For they are always comfortable.
The Kewps were cozy 'cause they're made so—
Began by being warm and stayed so.
Cried Santa, "Now what shall I do!
I simply can't get down that flue!"
Said Wag the Chief, "Dear sir, I hope
To solve the problem with a rope."

(And he did.)

Across the snow, o'er roofs they sped,
A million children visited
And stockings filled with speed surprising.
Said Santa, "This is paralyzing!
These Kewpies are most enterprising!"

Henceforth, no hesitance at all,
At every house with chimneys small,
They lower Santa with a will
Unto some handy window sill.
The gay old soul enjoyed the fun
And roared as through the air he spun.
His boots against the bricks go clumping,
His plump old person briskly bumping.
He cried, "I'm lively as a cat, now,
Why, I'm a reg'lar acrobat, now!
Those creaky joints were quite misleading.
'Twas only Kewpies I was needing!"

The gay old soul enjoyed the fun
And roared as through the air he spun

So, with that difficulty past,
The dear old saint got in at last.
No little child was then neglected,
But found at morn the joy expected.
New toys for every curly-head
And Kewpie dolls beside each bed.
"Well, Spry Assistants!" Santa said,
And hugged the Kewps with hearty cheers,
"If I can have these Kewpie dears,
I'll last another hundred years!"

And Kewpie dolls beside each bed

January 1914.

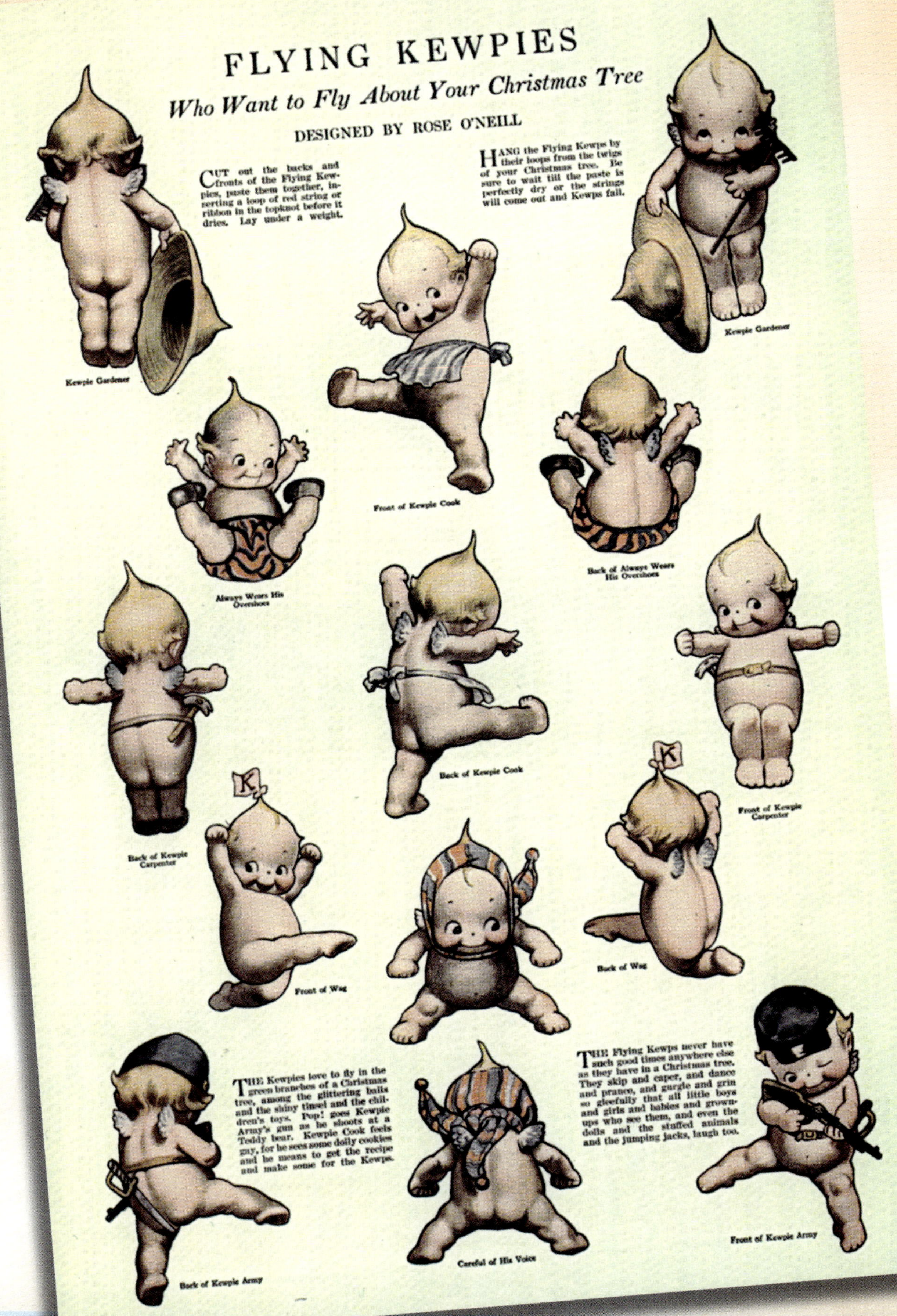

FLYING KEWPIES

Who Want to Fly About Your Christmas Tree

DESIGNED BY ROSE O'NEILL

CUT out the backs and fronts of the Flying Kewpies, paste them together, inserting a loop of red string or ribbon in the topknot before it dries. Lay under a weight.

HANG the Flying Kewps by their loops from the twigs of your Christmas tree. Be sure to wait till the paste is perfectly dry or the strings will come out and Kewps fall.

Kewpie Gardener

Front of Kewpie Cook

Kewpie Gardener

Always Wears His Overshoes

Back of Always Wears His Overshoes

Back of Kewpie Carpenter

Back of Kewpie Cook

Front of Kewpie Carpenter

Front of Wag

Back of Wag

THE Kewpies love to fly in the green branches of a Christmas tree, among the glittering balls and the shiny tinsel and the children's toys. Pop! goes Kewpie Army's gun as he shoots at a Teddy bear. Kewpie Cook feels gay, for he sees some dolly cookies and he means to get the recipe and make some for the Kewps.

THE Flying Kewps never have such good times anywhere else as they have in a Christmas tree. They skip and caper, and dance and prance, and gurgle and grin so gleefully that all little boys and girls and babies and grown-ups who see them, and even the dolls and the stuffed animals and the jumping jacks, laugh too.

Back of Kewpie Army

Careful of His Voice

Front of Kewpie Army

February 1914.

A KEWPIE VALENTINE

When you have finished the valentine, look on page 15 and read all about it

BY ROSE O'NEILL

THINK of it! A real Kewpie Valentine with three happy little Kewps peeping out!

First paste a stiff piece of paper on the back of the valentine to make the valentine stand up. Cut out the three ovals neatly. Then cut out the two Kewpie heads and paste the tabs on the back side of the valentine below the ovals so that each Kewpie head will peer out of its little window. Paste the ends of the blue ribbon behind the large oval on each side so that the middle Kewpie will be gaily flying through. Paste paper ovals on the back.

Cut out this Kewpie and paste the ends of his blue ribbon behind the valentine so that he will just be coming through the large oval.

VALENTINE'S DAY is one of the Kewpies' busiest seasons, for you see there are so many smiles and good wishes and love letters to carry around to all sorts of people. This year you are to put three of the Kewps in a valentine of your own to give away or to keep, just as you like. Wouldn't your grandma or grandpa like a Kewpie Valentine? And any little boy or girl that you know would be delighted, of course. With some of the Kewpie Kutouts that you have seen in the COMPANION before this, you can make other cunning valentines.

Your Kewpie Valentine

The Kewpish Adventures

Verses and Pictures by Rose O'Neill

Once, when the Kewps were forty-winking, dears,
And Ducky Daddles, too, was blinking, dears,
Where doll-beds in a stately toy-store, there,
Attracted them to make a joy-store, there;
The Kewpidoodle watched them warily,
Then rose and trotted off don't care-ily.

You see, he felt both odd and only-ish,
As well as just a trifle lonely-ish

The Kewpidoodle was thinking considerably.

376

The *Kewpidoodle Dog* from *Good Housekeeping*, April 1915.

of the Kewpidoodle

For other dogs to race and wrestle with,
To roll upon the grass and nestle with,
The poor thing craved canine society,
Such quadrupedic inebriety
As some old shoe shared disputatiously
With lively dogs inclined pugnaciously,
Who'd pull and haul at it unlawfully
And show their teeth, while growling awfully!

His life, he thought, was too meticulous,
Too namby-pamby and ridiculous,
Too pampered, petted, snug, and poodle-ish,
For one so brave and Kewpidoodle-ish—
In fact, he hated to be toodle-ish!
Of St. Bernards he dreamed ambitiously:
He'd go and *be* one, surreptitiously!

But on the road he met
His Yellowship,
A battered dog inclined
to fellowship,

With whom he tarried round a bit, you see,
So if somebody had a fit, you see,
He'd be there on the spot to save 'em quick;
(The Yellow Dog's advice was "Lave 'em quick!"
Himself, he said, had found that friendliness
Could culminate in tin-can endliness!)

The Kewpie dog now saw
a basket, dears,
And though the Lady
did not ask it, dears,

The Yellow dog was so surprised.

377

He started
off with it
most helpfully,
And 'stead of thanks,
she chased him
yelpfully!
This so upset his equanimity,
It so disturbed his soul's sublimity,
That over him there crept a droopishness
That made him long for Home—and Kewpishness!

A bulldog's fearsome at his happiest,
Words can't describe him at his scrappiest,
With battling eye, triumphant bragginess,
And utter lack of pleasant wagginess.

The poor, scared Kewpidoodle smiled at him,
Which made that bulldog simply wild at him.
"Am I the sport of you riffraff?" he roared;
"Am I that sight that makes dogs laugh?" he roared.

The Kewpidoodle's intentions were so kindly.

378

Good Housekeeping, July 1918.
Shirley Karaba Collection.

The Kewpies and Liberty's Birthday

By Rose O'Neill

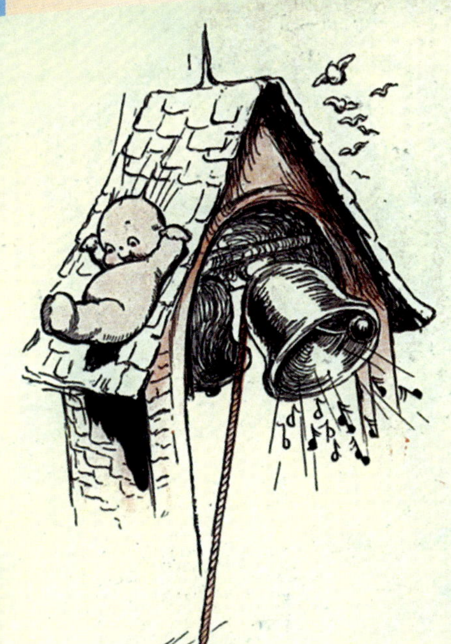

One summer day, the Kewpies were rather startled by Wag, the Kewpie Chief, who came at a terrific speed carrying a calendar with a large 4 marking the 4th. of July. He had just found out that this meant Liberty's Birthday and he felt that something must be done about it. The Kewps agreed emphatically, and, in a few minutes, the joy-bells were ringing.

The Kewpie Cook borrowed somebody's kitchen and began a birthday cake, while the Kewp who is always-careful-of-his-complexion brought more than a hundred candles to put on it.

46

Then the Information Kewp looked up Liberty's location in his book and they all set sail across the Bay, carrying the cake. Some rowed, some sang patriotic songs.
Some were attached to toy balloons to accelerate speed.
Of course, the little Mer-Kewps swam. Some old-fashioned fish were quite surprised at the party. The birth-day cake was remarkable, going over the water with all its candles lighted
BAIT
INFORMATION
BEDLOE'S ISLAND
47

Good Housekeeping, July 1918.
Shirley Karaba Collection.

Good Housekeeping, July 1918.
Shirley Karaba Collection.

Liberty seemed to enjoy her
birthday party very much. Some
Kewps held up her torch while
she ate her cake, and others
took the occasion to tidy her up
a bit with whisk-brooms and
sweep and scrub her pedestal.
They were all of the opinion
that it was a more agreeable
4th. than if they had all been
blown up by fire-crackers, and
everything was delightful-
Hoping you are the same
I am Kewpishly yours,
Rose O'Neill.
MANY HAPPY RETURNS OF THE
48

The Ladies' Home Journal, May 1926.

The Ladies' HOME JOURNAL

May, 1926

Kewpieville

By ROSE O'NEILL

Kewpies make quite a specialty of getting little animals cosied after they have been bothered by hunters.

Now in Kewpieville, of course, there is no such thing as a tiresome person (always excepting dear little Uncle Hob). All the dogs are puppies and all the cats are kittens.

But when a regular grown-up Tabby occasionally drops in to Kewpieville they make her as comfortable as possible and the Mayor entertains her with cream, catnip and conundrums.

Chickadees are great chums of the Kewps, who call them "Kewpidees" because of their rounded conformation. They have the most agreeable conversations together.

There is almost always a band going on in the town.
And Kewpieville loves elections and processions.

Uncle Hob had a marked objection to bands, processions and joy in general.

Nearly every day somebody is elected to the office of Chief Joy-dispenser and crowned with a wreath of little bells (until everybody in town has got elected; then they begin over again).

Scootles, the Baby Tourist (sitting on a housetop), had the gratification of seeing her friend, Johnny McKewp, made Chief Joy-dispenser.

Hoping you are the same,
I am Kewpishly yours,

Rose O'Neill

The Ladies' Home Journal, September 1926.

The Ladies' HOME JOURNAL

Kewpieville

By ROSE O'NEILL

One nice thing about Kewpieville is that when a Kewpie goes to the Pet Animile Shop he doesn't have to pick out anything. The little animal picks out the Kewpie. This saves the wear and tear of rathering. The prices are moderate—just a few hugs or kisses.

When Katy O'Kewp was looking in the window, the Butterfly Cat picked her immediately and Katy had many a fine ride.

But when the Butterfly Cat had a bunch of Butterfly Kittens, Uncle Hob said it was going too far, and got the scissors. He said that wings on cats weren't natural, and for his part, he didn't propose to put up with it.

So the Mayor and the Poli
had the Kewpieville Taik
take off Uncle Hob's ow
wings for the afternoon. Thi
showed him a thing or two.

After he got his wings back in the evening, he sat quite peacefully with a Butterfly Kitten on his knee.

The Baby Tourist, who is a great traveler, wrote this letter home on the subject: It is naturable to be as lovely as possible. Kewpishly yours, Scootles."

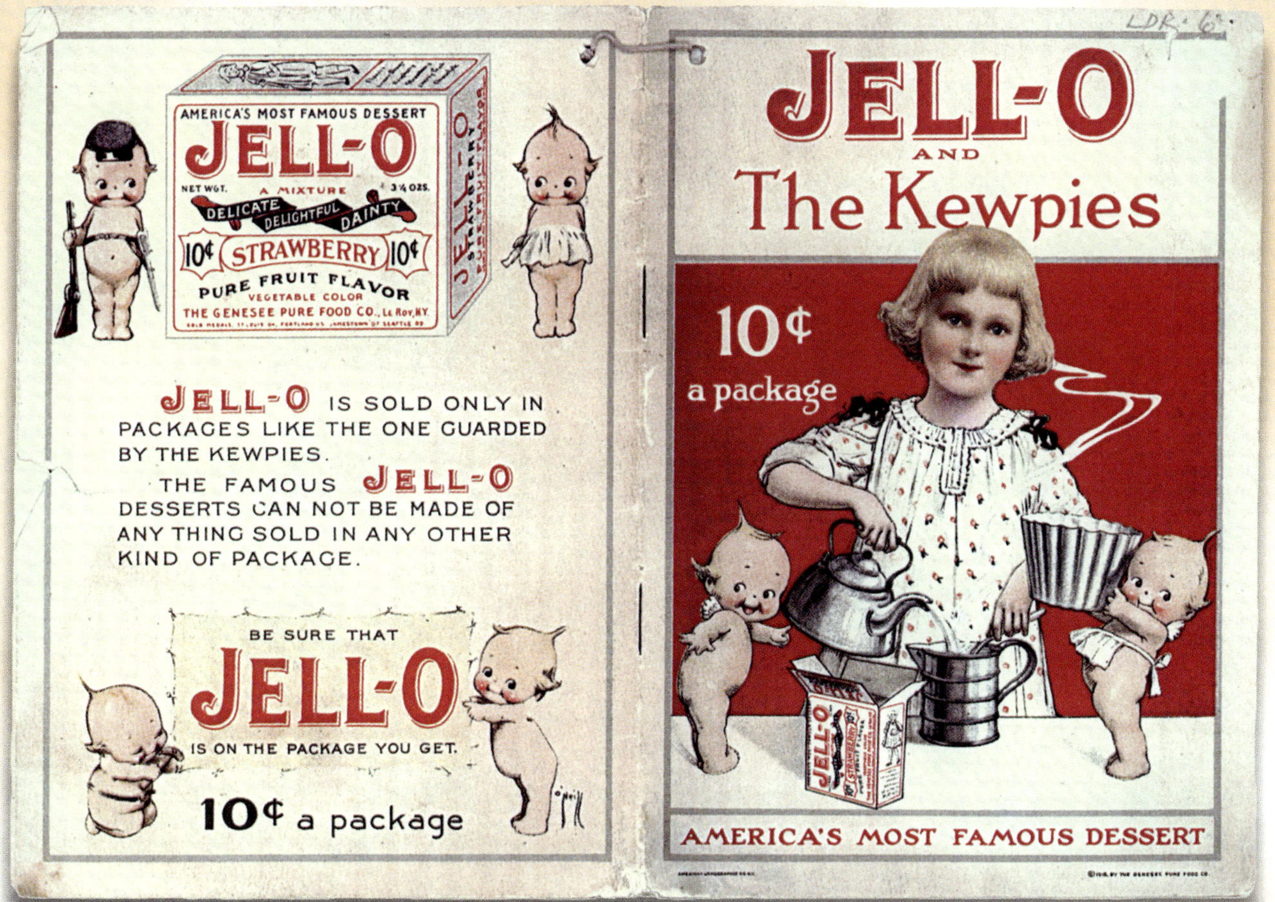

AMERICA'S MOST FAMOUS DESSERT
JELL-O
NET WGT. A MIXTURE 3¼ OZS.
DELICATE DELIGHTFUL DAINTY
10¢ STRAWBERRY 10¢
PURE FRUIT FLAVOR
VEGETABLE COLOR
THE GENESEE PURE FOOD CO., Le Roy, N.Y.
JELL-O IS SOLD ONLY IN PACKAGES LIKE THE ONE GUARDED BY THE KEWPIES.
THE FAMOUS JELL-O DESSERTS CAN NOT BE MADE OF ANY THING SOLD IN ANY OTHER KIND OF PACKAGE.
BE SURE THAT
JELL-O
IS ON THE PACKAGE YOU GET.
10¢ a package
JELL-O
AND
The Kewpies
10¢
a package
AMERICA'S MOST FAMOUS DESSERT

Advertising booklet for Jell-o, 1915. *Shirley Karaba Collection.*

MARION HARLAND'S PINEAPPLE BAVARIAN CREAM
DELMONICO DESSERT
JELL-O FRUIT COCKTAIL
CREAM FIG PUDDING
JELL-O RELISH
MRS. HERRICK'S CHOCOLATE CHARLOTTE
RASPBERRY JELL-O
NEAPOLITAN JELL-O
ROMAN SPONGE
9
10

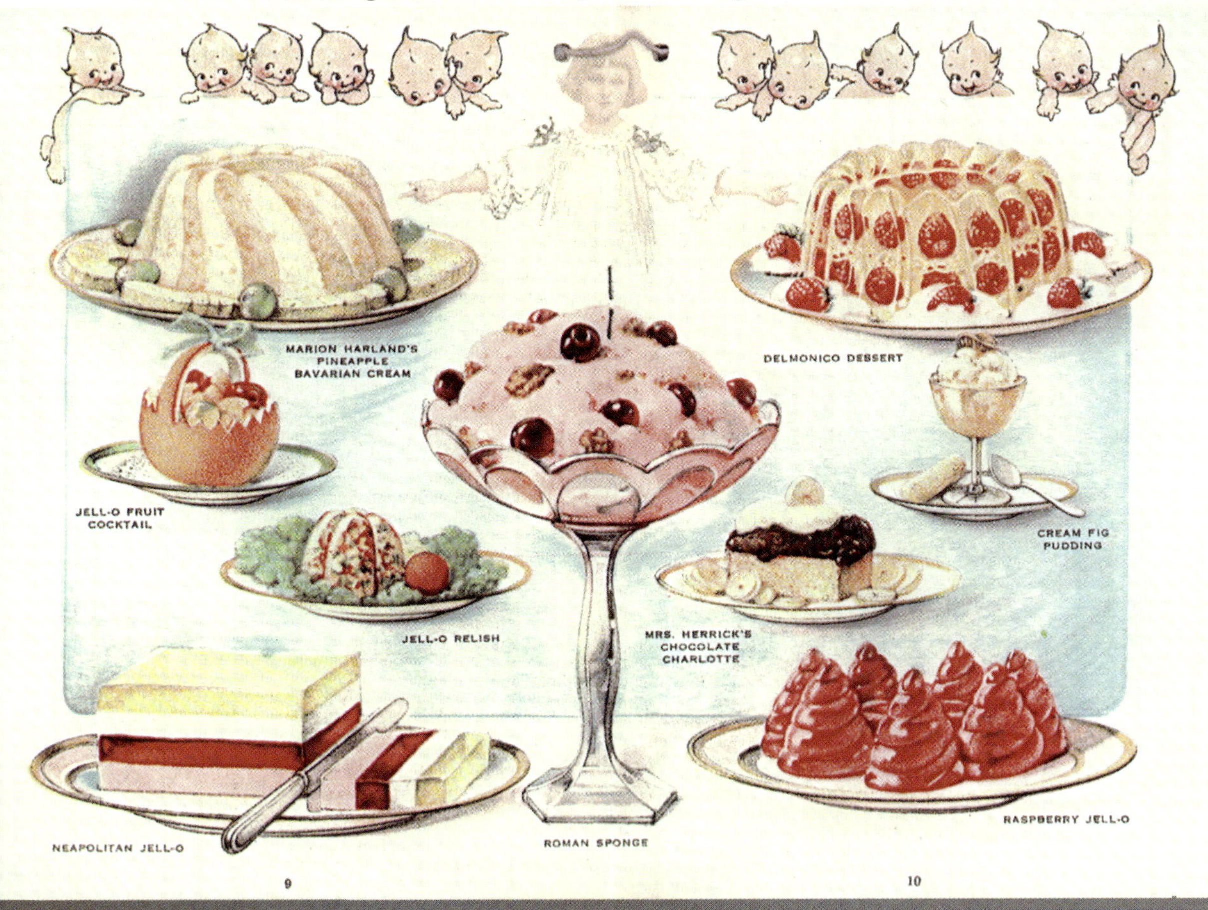

Pictorial Review for March, 1919

70

O'Neill

They Wanted Jell-O

Do you remember the dreadful disappointment it used to be in the old days at home when mother brought on for dessert some baked apples or pieplant pie, or something else that was too common, and you had expected ice cream or shortcake at least?

Now the little folks want Jell-O, and it is so delicious, refreshing, pure and wholesome, so "economical" and so easily prepared, that there is no reason why the little tots or anybody else should be disappointed in their dessert.

Creamy Desserts

That do not require any cream at all for making them, nor eggs or sugar, are made in perfection of Jell-O—and of course they do not have to be cooked.

To give you the best possible idea of "the Jell-O way" we will send you, free, a copy of the latest Jell-O Book, which gives full information on the subject, if you will send us your name and address.

In every case of sickness or convalescence there is a period when feeding is a most important factor, and often it is found that Jell-O is the one particular dish which satisfies the craving for something refreshing and revives the weakened appetite.

Jell-O is made in six pure fruit flavors: Strawberry, Raspberry, Lemon, Orange, Cherry, Chocolate. At any grocer's, **2** packages for **25** cents.

THE GENESEE PURE FOOD COMPANY,
Le Roy, N. Y., and Bridgeburg, Ont.

The *Kewpies* and other Rose O'Neill artwork were used to advertise Jell-O in many different magazines during the 1910s. This ad showing two children by Rose O'Neill is from *Pictorial Review*, March 1919.

Joseph L. Kallus

Even without the participation of Joseph L. Kallus, there would no doubt have been *Kewpie* figurines and dolls. Another sculptor may have done the original three-dimensional renderings of *Kewpie* and presented them in an appealing manner, but the *Kewpie* "story" would have been far different than it has been without the creative genius of Mr. Kallus.

The popularity of Rose O'Neill's saucy little *Kewpie* drawings in magazines from 1909–1910 created a demand for commercial manufacture of items bearing the likeness of *Kewpie*. There was an opportunity to develop *Kewpie* books, comic strips, lamps, dishes, postcards, figurines, dolls, jewelry, and many other kinds of merchandise. Rose O'Neill would not have been able to produce all the models and samples that mass merchandising required.

One of the first distributors to show an interest in the *Kewpie* properties was Geo. Borgfeldt & Co. This company was formed in 1881 as a partnership with George Borgfeldt, Marcell Kahle and Joseph L. Kahle. The purpose of the firm was to import dolls, toys, figurines, and novelty items from Europe for distribution to the American market. Branch offices of Borgfeldt & Co. were established in New York, Canada and all over Europe, particularly in Germany, the center of the doll and toy manufacturing industry. George Borgfeldt resigned as president of the firm in 1900 and was succeeded by Marcell Kahle. After the death of Kahle in 1909, Fred Kolb became president of the company. In 1912, Kolb entered negotiations with Rose O'Neill to produce a variety of *Kewpie* figurines and dolls. They decided to hire an American assistant to render designs from Rose O'Neill drawings of *Kewpie*.

Joseph L. Kallus, a student at the Fine Arts College of Pratt Institute in Brooklyn, applied for the position of sculptor and was interviewed by Kolb and O'Neill. Kallus, who was born in Hungary February 12, 1893, made some rough modeling sketches from Rose O'Neill's drawings and was hired to execute *Kewpies* for manufacture in Germany.

It has always been the practice in the doll industry for a designer (in this case Rose O'Neill) to initiate the idea for a doll and to establish a rough parameter of the conceived product and to obtain assistance in the actual modeling and casting of the doll. Then the original designer offers suggestions, changes and approves the final product. Kallus worked with O'Neill in designing the first *Kewpie* figurines and dolls that were to be produced in porcelain in Germany in several factories in which Borgfeldt was affiliated. Among these factories was J.D. Kestner, Gebr. Voigt, Hermann Voigt, and Hertwig & Co. *Kewpies* were also made in celluloid by Carl Standfuss and in cloth by Margarete Steiff.

Self-portrait of Joseph L. Kallus.

Fred Kolb and Rose O'Neill were delighted with the work that Joseph Kallus was completing on the *Kewpie* project. Kolb also retained Kallus to design other dolls while he continued his studies at Pratt Institute.

Dorothy Gregory Moffett was a fellow art student in the Pratt classes attended by Kallus in 1912. In 1974, during legal proceedings to protect the *Kewpie* copyrights, Moffett submitted an affidavit in which she told about the first time she saw the *Kewpie* dolls:

> Mr. Kallus brought three *Kewpie* doll heads to class, and he passed them around and explained the work he was doing on them. This demonstration occurred in the Max Herman illustration class. I did not know at the time of the demonstration that these were *Kewpie* dolls. I knew only that that they were different from the dolls we were used to seeing. They had no hair, but they had a small topknot on a symmetrically round head to depict the caricature of a child, which distinguished them from anything I had ever seen in dolls. It was not until I saw *Kewpie* illustrations published in *Good Housekeeping Magazine*, *Ladies' Home Journal* [sic] and other periodicals that I came to know that the dolls, which Mr. Kallus had demonstrated to the class, were the original sculptures of illustrations drawn and originally conceived by Rose O'Neill from which *Kewpie* dolls were made.
>
> My clear recollection is that the doll heads, which Mr. Kallus demonstrated to the class at that time, were handmade samples in plaster of Paris. Mr. Kallus explained to the instructor (Max Herman) the work he had done on these heads and asked for comment and criticism. I was quite interested in this incident and have retained a recollection of it over the years.
>
> ...To the best of my knowledge and belief, Mr. Kallus and I are the sole surviving students of that class.

Doll design gave Joseph L. Kallus a career that he had not considered when he first entered Pratt Institute on a scholarship. The bisque dolls and figurines of *Kewpie* were probably produced in Germany during 1913 and 1914 and likely again in the 1920s after World War I. In 1916, Kallus himself founded the Rex Doll Co. to produce composition *Kewpie* dolls, as supplies from Germany were halted by the war. Borgfeldt, who controlled all production rights to *Kewpie* dolls and figurines, distributed these dolls. With permission from Borgfeldt, the Rex Doll Co. also made a line of composition *Kewpie* dolls that were distributed by the Tip Top Toy Co., a supplier of carnival prizes. (It should be remembered that carnival prizes were a much higher grade of merchandise in 1916 than they are in more recent times.)

In 1918, Kallus received the first of many copyrights on his own doll designs. His first character doll was *Baby Bundie*. That year, at about age 24, Kallus attempted to secure an assignment for the war effort. He had several of his instructors at Pratt Institute, among them Frederick T. Baker and O.W. Beck, and Frank Vincent DuMond, an instructor at the Art Students' League of New York (where Kallus had also studied), submit letters of reference to Charles Dana Gibson, the famous illustrator and creator of the "Gibson Girl," who was Chairman of Pictorial Publicity in New York for the war effort. Kallus was not able to secure a position pertaining to his art background, so he trained for fire observation during World War I.

From 1919 to 1921, Kallus was president of the Mutual Doll Co., a firm that made composition *Kewpies*; *Baby Bundie* dolls; and *Bo-Fair, Dollie* and *Vanitie* dolls that had specially designed socket joints. Kallus resigned from Mutual in 1921. (The president of a doll company is not necessarily the owner of the firm.)

In 1922, Kallus established the Cameo Doll Co., which lasted in one form or another until 1982 when he assigned the rights to control his doll and toy properties to Jesco, Inc. of Monrovia, California. Most of the dolls and toy animals manufactured by Cameo until after World War II were made of composition and segmented wood joints. Cameo made *Kewpies* for Borgfeldt and introduced the Kallus designs *Baby Bo Kaye* and *Little Annie Rooney*. *Little Annie Rooney* was the creation of Jack Collins, who wrote and illustrated comic strips for newspapers. The

Kallus *Little Annie Rooney* was made as an all-bisque figure and as a fully-jointed composition doll.

The Cameo Doll Products Company was located in Port Allegheny, Pennsylvania, from 1933 until 1968, when the molds for dolls were taken over by the Strombecker Corporation of Chicago. In October 1934, a fire almost devastated the entire Cameo plant during its busiest season. After rebuilding, Cameo also manufactured dolls for other companies, which packaged them in boxes with their own company names, most notably the Effanbee Doll Corporation while Noma Electric owned it in the late 1940s. Even now in McKean County, Pennsylvania, where Kallus' Port Allegheny plant was located, and in adjacent Potter County, there seems to be an abundance of Cameo *Kewpies* in antique shops and other places where collectibles are sold. These examples must have come from employees of Cameo, as the population of this region of Pennsylvania has always been very small.

President Franklin D. Roosevelt summoned Joseph L. Kallus to Washington, D.C., in 1933 as a representative of small industrial firms in Pennsylvania. Kallus consulted with the President to suggest the most feasible methods of bringing the Depression economy back to normal production.

When Rose O'Neill died in 1944, the rights to produce *Kewpie, Scootles* and *Ho-Ho* were granted to Joseph L. Kallus in an indirect manner. Before her death, Rose O'Neill had attempted to transfer the rights to her creations to Kallus. In 1947, all trademark, patent and copyrights to the *Kewpie* properties were assigned to Joseph L. Kallus by Paul E. O'Neill, Rose's nephew and heir. Paul E. O'Neill renewed the copyright for the book *Kewpie and the Runaway Baby* in 1955 and Kallus later requested from Paul E. O'Neill's wife that these rights be assigned to him, as he wanted "to protect the good will and name of Rose O'Neill and her *Kewpie* creation." Kallus later obtained the rights to other O'Neill properties, such as *Scootles* and *Ho-Ho.*

Mr. Kallus spent a great deal of his energy in his later years licensing *Kewpie* designs and entering litigation with the various firms and individuals to whom he had licensed the right to produce *Kewpie* and other O'Neill designs. In 1976, at age 83, Kallus suffered a great personal and professional loss when thieves entered his basement in Brooklyn and stole a large number of *Kewpie* models and designs, including patent materials from two safes that were stored there. The police did not understand the value of these things. Detective Robert Hall of the 67th Precinct said to the *New York Times* reporter, "The dolls were probably handmade and looked pretty, with pretty clothes." Kallus claimed that many of his original models of *Kewpie*, the original *Scootles*, his handmade *Joy*, his version of Disney's *Mickey Mouse,* the originals of *Howdy Doody, Superman* and *Pinocchio* were also gone forever. Imagine how valuable these models would be today in a museum.

In 1960, Kallus approached the American Character Doll Co. in an effort to have that firm produce *Kewpies* under license to Cameo. American Character was not able to deal with Kallus' blunt style after he accused the company of attempting to copy some of his original concepts.

It is imperative that a copyright owner protects his property. If he fails to do so, he could lose the rights he owns. During the 1960s, other doll companies and novelty manufacturers, particularly those operating in Asia, were plagiarizing Rose O'Neill and Joseph Kallus *Kewpie* designs. Kallus knew that he had to protect the rights that he had gained from the O'Neill estate if he wanted to continue to own them.

Strombecker of Chicago began producing *Kewpie* dolls under license to Kallus and Cameo in 1969 and encouraged Mr. Kallus to permit greetings cards companies to print Rose O'Neill's artwork because it would help promote interest in *Kewpie,* which was more popular than it had been for many years. (American Greetings Corporation of Cleveland, Ohio, had a line of *Kewpie* stationery products in the early 1970s.) Strombecker and Cameo terminated their agreement by 1973 because Kallus was not granted the privilege of approving samples of the dolls that the company would produce. A licensor usually maintains this right to control the integrity of his copyrighted properties.

In 1972, Knickerbocker Toy Co, Inc. approached Mr. Kallus for permission to license characters that were controlled by Cameo. A contract was awarded, but it only lasted about a year. At the same time Joseph L. Kallus made an agreement with Kutsuwa Co., Ltd. of Osaka, Japan, to license several *Kewpie* properties.

In 1973, Milton Bradley, Inc., under the Amsco division of the company, began to manufacture *Kewpies* in vinyl. The relationship between Milton Bradley and Cameo was severed in 1976 over conflicts in royalty payments and the fact that the company did not mark its doll packages in accordance with its contract with Kallus.

Again in 1980, Kallus tried to interest Knickerbocker in manufacturing *Kewpie* dolls, but the company was afraid to deal with him after it was known that he had problems with Strombecker and Milton Bradley, which were assumed to be more the fault of an aging and irascible Kallus than of the doll companies.

By 1980, it was becoming more and more difficult to protect *Kewpie* copyright infringements. Unscrupulous individuals and companies were printing *Kewpie* postcards and other *Kewpie* likenesses and making dolls that looked like an authentic *Kewpie* and selling these things both commercially and on an individual basis to collectors. Others made unauthorized *Kewpie* dolls and products to sell because they lacked business experience, education and sophistication. All of this would cause potential problems for those who wanted to manufacture genuine *Kewpie* dolls and other products and to Kallus who wanted to protect his rights and licenses.

In 1982, Jesco Imports, Inc. of Monrovia, California, began negotiations with Mr. Kallus for *Kewpie* licenses. Jesco Imports, Inc., begun in 1972 by James E. Skahill as the James E. Skahill Company, was a toy and import business. The company was incorporated in 1976 as Jesco Imports, Inc. It handled such doll lines as Italocremona, Migliorati, Corolle, Famosa, and about 20 others. Mr. Skahill, who was born on a farm in Iowa in 1925, had started in the toy business in 1957 as a sales representative for Amsco (who made *Kewpies* during the 1970s). By the time he was negotiating the *Kewpie* rights with Mr. Kallus, Skahill had been involved in the doll and toy import and distribution business for 25 years. Kallus was impressed with Jesco's business philosophies. Jesco Imports, Inc. was committed to developing a business based on quality toys for the quality toy market. Joseph Kallus said that he was not as interested in making money at his age as he was in continuing the traditions of excellence that had always been associated with *Kewpie* and with Cameo. Kallus agreed to assign all licensing rights to *Kewpie* and other Cameo designs to Jesco Imports, Inc.

After Kallus had concluded the initial phase of his business arrangement with Jesco, he was injured in a traffic accident and died suddenly. Mr. Kallus' daughter and heir, Rita Abraham, wished to continue with her father's intentions and she formally and legally licensed the *Kewpie*® and Cameo properties to Jesco Imports, Inc.

Joseph L. Kallus had been involved with sculpting and manufacturing *Kewpies* for seventy years. This must be a record in the toy industry.

Coloring book by Saalfield, #9546, 1966. Copyright by Jos. L. Kallus.

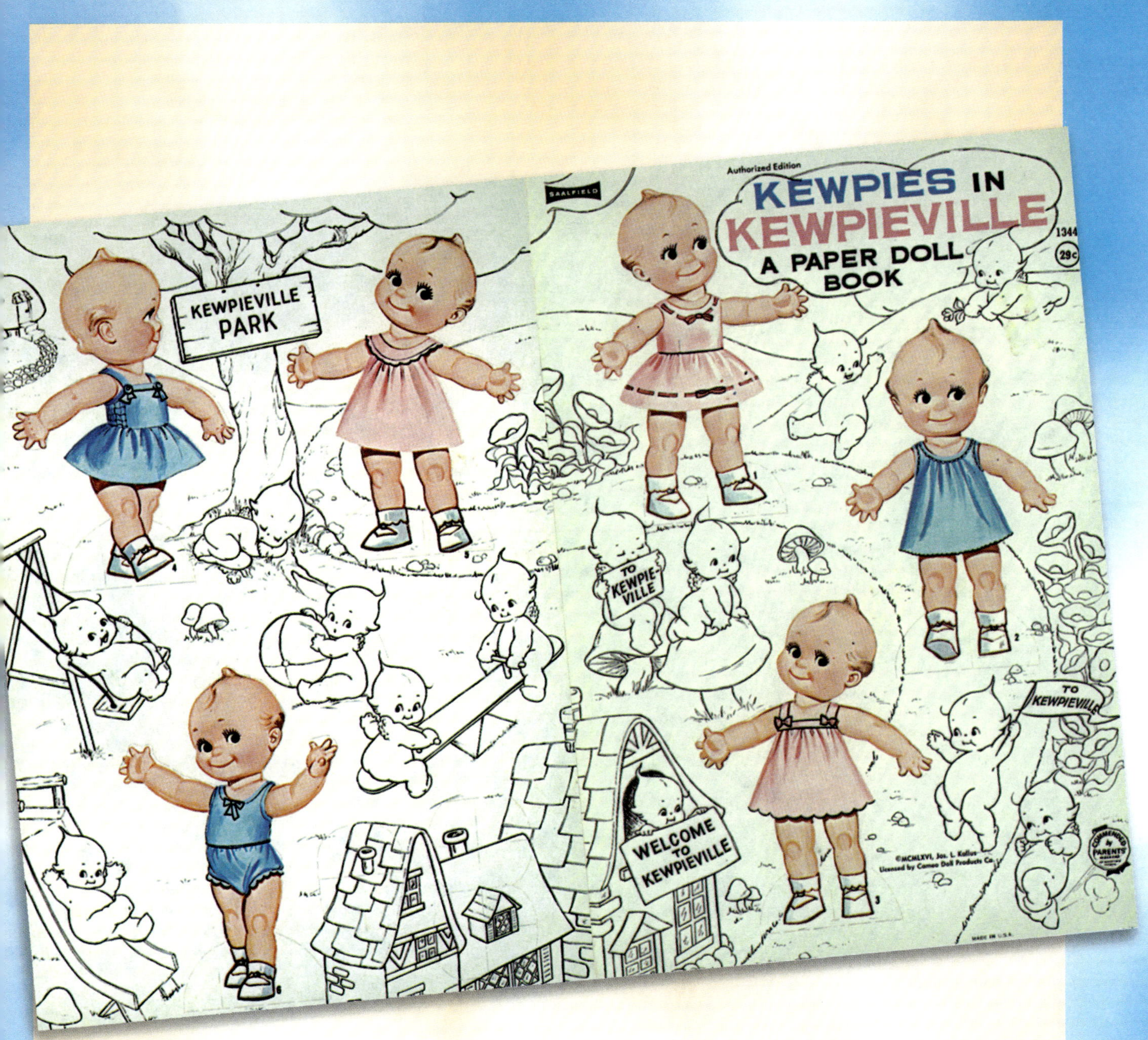

Paper doll book by Saalfield, #1344, 1966.
Copyright by Jos. L. Kallus.

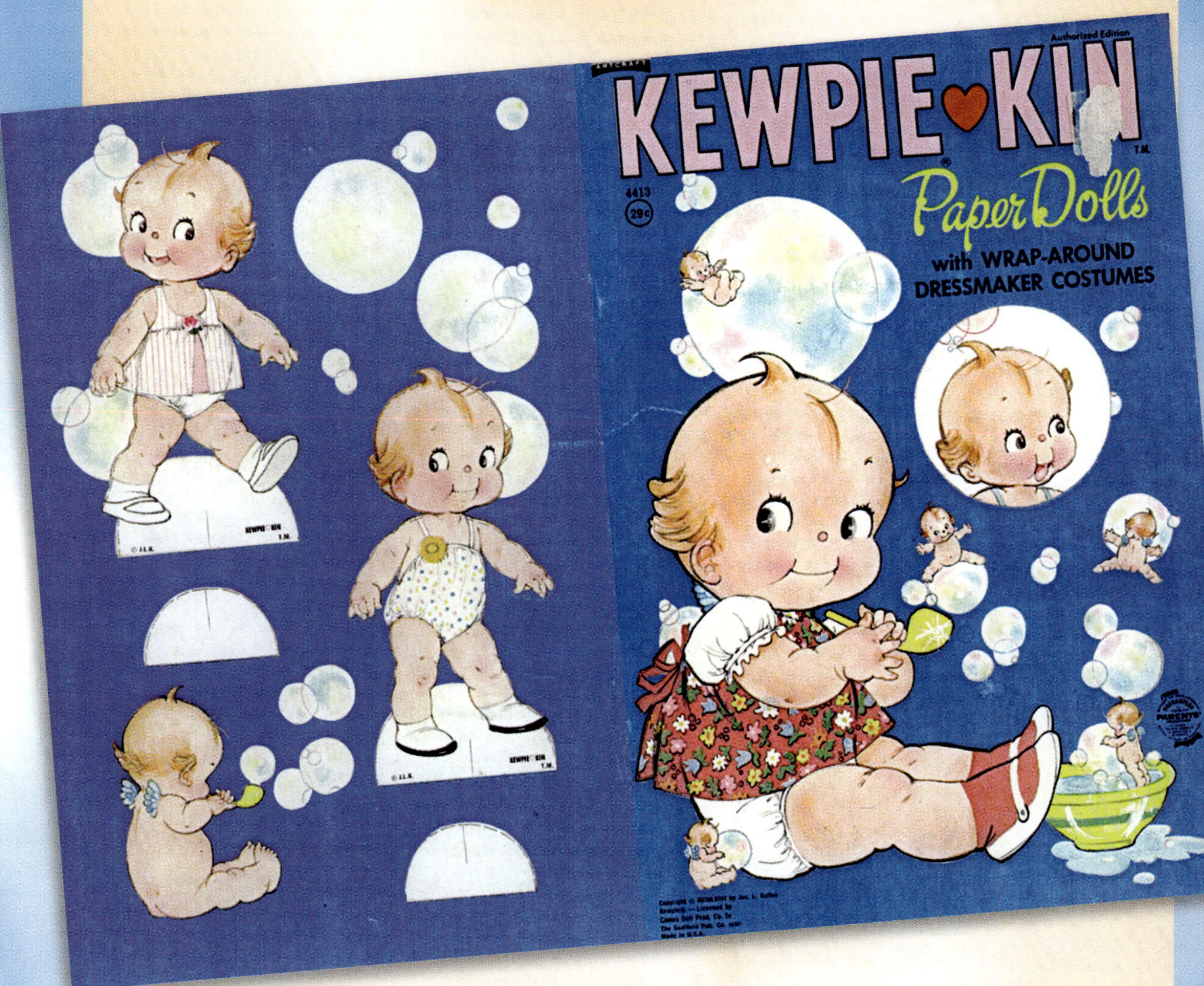

Paper doll book by Artcraft (Saalfield), #4413, 1967. Copyright by Jos. L. Kallus.

Paper doll book by Artcraft (Saalfield), #4488, 1967, a variation of #4413. Copyright by Jos. L. Kallus.

The first page of the Artcraft book, which is seen though a glassine window on the front cover, is on heavy stock like the covers. #4488.

Die-cut "facsimile" storybook by Merrimac Publishing, 1983.

Jesco, Inc.

Rita Abraham, the daughter of Joseph L. Kallus, retained the ownership of *Kewpie* and Cameo products after her father's death, and licensed the properties to Jesco Imports, Inc. of Monrovia, California. Jesco made *Kewpies* in its own facilities in California from American components using the original Cameo molds. James E. Skahill, CEO of Jesco, and his partner, Nancy Villaseñor-Cordaro, President of Jesco Imports, Inc., brought the *Kewpie* dolls back as high quality products, which they had not been since the days of Kallus' own Cameo Doll Company.

Jesco released its first *Kewpie* in 1983. This, a tribute to Joseph L. Kallus, was a re-issue of the 27-inch (69cm) Cameo *Kewpie*, which had been manufactured by Strombecker. The special Jesco *Kewpie* for collectors was slightly smaller than the original vinyl version because it was cast from Kallus' original molds rather than using the stock body and legs of the Strombecker doll. The 1983 dolls also included a set of 16-inch (41cm) dolls called "Yesterday's *Kewpie*" that was dressed in outfits from the past and "*Kewpie* Goes ...," a 12-inch (31cm) series in various theme-oriented designs. The larger of these two sets of *Kewpies* were modeled after designs that Cameo issued in 1961; the smaller ones had clothing designed by Shirley Pepys. The first Jesco *Kewpies* met with the objectives of Joseph L. Kallus: "To make *Kewpies* available for the enjoyment of children and to satisfy the *Kewpie* hunger of collectors."

James E. and Marie Skahill of Jesco Imports, Inc.

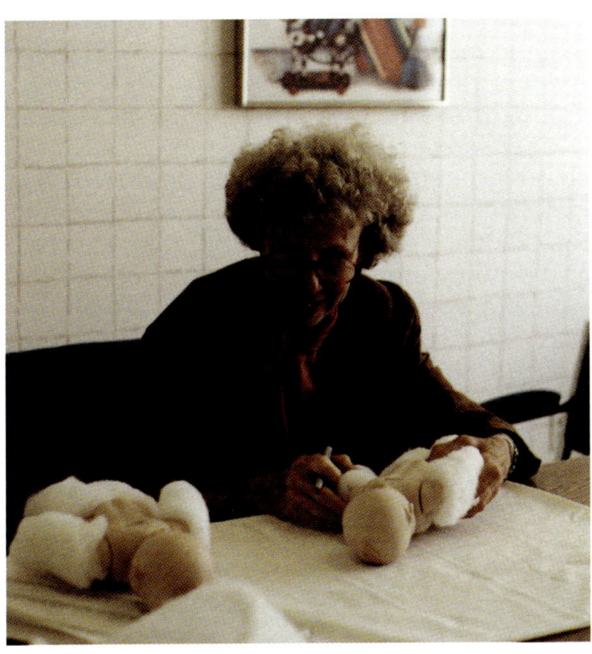

Joseph L. Kallus' daughter Rita Abraham signing a 14-inch (36cm) porcelain Kewpie for a Collector's Day promotion for the home shopping television network, QVC, in 1994 at the Jesco offices. *Courtesy of Jesco Imports, Inc.*

Jesco Imports, Inc. made *Kewpies* from 1983 through 1995 under license from Rita Abraham, the daughter of Joseph L. Kallus and the holder of the *Kewpie* copyright. During the 1990s, Rita Abraham presented *Kewpie* dolls on QVC, a home shopping outlet on television, and acted as spokeswoman on behalf of Jesco Imports, Inc. In 1996, Jesco became a licensing agent for *Kewpie* and ended doll production. In October 2002, Jesco became the owner of the *Kewpie* copyrights, as they relate to consumer products.

Tom Skahill, a consultant for Jesco, explained the licensing process: A contract is granted to a Licensee after all details of the potential product are approved. This is to maintain the integrity of the *Kewpie* image. Fees and royalties may be charged. The contracts are an exclusive arrangement. Only one company may produce *Kewpie* or another Cameo product in the form for which the license is granted. For example, under the exclusive arrangement, only one company is granted the right to produce a high-quality limited edition collector's doll; only one company is granted a mass-market product license; and only one manufacturer can produce a direct-response marketing doll.

In many respects, Jesco has done more to develop and promote *Kewpie* properties than anything that has happened since the days of Geo. Borgfeldt & Co. before World War I. Beginning in 1983, Jesco launched an extensive line of *Kewpie* dolls made of vinyl in the United States at a time when it was becoming the normal procedure in the American doll industry to manufacture dolls made of plastic and vinyl materials in Asia, especially in China. The first Jesco *Kewpies* were of two types. One was a line of nostalgic *Kewpies* that were similar to the ones that Joseph Kallus made in his Cameo factory and then licensed to other doll manufacturers from the 1950s through the 1970s. Jesco's first *Kewpie* is the largest size doll it made—the 25-inch (64cm) "Joseph L. Kallus Memorial *Kewpie*." The "Yesterday's *Kewpie*" line that was dressed in traditional and old-fashioned costumes was also reminiscent of the dolls that Mr. Kallus produced in his own factories. The other line of *Kewpie* dolls from Jesco featured *Kewpie* as a contemporary character. The group called "*Kewpie* Goes..." included dolls whose names describe their persona, such as "...to a Slumber Party," "...to a Birthday Party," and "...on a Picnic."

During the 1990s, there were many different doll characters made featuring *Kewpie*. These dolls came in sizes of 8in (20cm), 12in (31cm), 16in (41cm) and showed *Kewpie* dressed as brides and grooms, clowns, fairy tale characters, bunnies, flappers from the "Roaring 20s," and even as Santa Claus. There were both white and black versions of *Kewpie*. The costumes for the Jesco *Kewpies* were among the very best in the American doll industry.

Jesco also manufactured other Rose O'Neill and Cameo designs. By 1984, there was a line of *Scootles* dolls and the Kallus *Miss Peep* baby dolls. Other Kallus designs, notably *Peanut*, followed. By the 1990s, there was a *Kewpie Gal* (with molded hair), Rose O'Neill's *Ho-Ho* and children's china dishes with *Kewpie* designs on them. At the same time that Jesco was expanding the range of *Kewpie* dolls it was also promoting the *Katie* fashion doll and importing Hermann mohair teddy bears for the collector.

In the period after 1996, when Jesco concentrated on licensing *Kewpies*, some of the very best designs ever have been produced. Examples of these are the *Kewpies* in sunsuits from Effanbee and the porcelain collector's dolls from the Danbury Mint. In recent years, some of the most respected and valuable *Kewpies* ever have been available. A good example of these is the felt *Kewpies* from R. John Wright Dolls. And *Kewpie* has come almost back to its very inception as a three-dimensional product with the new *Kewpie* figurines from The German Doll Company. These figurines are made from original molds dating back prior to World War I when Joseph L. Kallus first sculpted dolls and figurines of Rose O'Neill's *Kewpie*.

Kewpie is one of the most innovative and clever artistic renderings ever produced. The simplicity of the little nude, winged sprite that Rose O'Neill first drew is still alive and still entertaining and amusing people just as it did almost a hundred years ago. Rose O'Neill was right: "The world needs to laugh, or at least to smile more than it does."

Chapter 2

Kewpie Action Figures and Novelties

Geo. Borgfeldt & Co. of New York obtained the right to manufacture three-dimensional likenesses of *Kewpie* from Rose O'Neill. In 1912, Joseph L. Kallus was hired to develop figurines and dolls of *Kewpie* based on Rose O'Neill's popular magazine drawings.

It is the usual business procedure in these arrangements for the company that will wholesale the product to develop certain types of examples that it thinks will have a wide retail market. In other words, the main reason that the charming collectibles from the past that collectors now crave were originally manufactured was for the purpose of making money. Therefore, *Kewpie* dolls and figurines that Borgfeldt distributed were not the creative expression of Rose O'Neill. She created the original ideas as illustrations and for the three-dimensional *Kewpie* works received a minimum royalty for each one sold.

From about 1913 to about 1918, *Kewpies* were marketed in the thousands, if not in the millions. Miss O'Neill received a lot of money from the production of the dolls and figurines that Borgfeldt distributed to retailers from their suppliers in German porcelain (and celluloid) factories. Joseph L. Kallus was probably paid a salary or a fee for each *Kewpie* item that he created from the O'Neill drawings. Miss O'Neill may have had the right to approve all designs executed by Kallus and placed into production. But it is unlikely that she constantly exercised those rights after the initial stages of the business agreements between herself, Borgfeldt and Kallus, during which time she had approved the first of Kallus' *Kewpie* samples. In her January 1914 article in *Woman's Home Companion*, O'Neill indicated that she went "from factory to factory" in Germany supervising *Kewpie* production and that she personally "pulled several hundreds out of one yawning furnace" while she was instructing German workers. By 1914, she wished to promote *Kewpie* production and to clearly establish the fact that *Kewpie* was her "invention."

Rose O'Neill's *Kewpie* drawings and her renderings of children were among the best illustrations of their day. Based on the volume of drawings found as magazine pages during the early 20th century, she produced her work quickly, although she did not shirk in including as many details in them as possible. These early magazine stories and drawings show most of the *Kewpies* that were produced as figurines and dolls before World War I in all their various guises and characterizations, from gardeners to soldiers to sun-bonneted babies.

The drawings were probably translated into figurines and dolls in this manner: The Borgfeldt company would determine if it could market a certain style of doll or figurine. Principals within the company would then study Rose O'Neill's published or unpublished drawings and predict which renderings would translate well into an item, such as a *Kewpie Traveler.* Then Joseph Kallus would be commissioned to sculpt *Kewpie Traveler* in clay. From the clay model, a plaster mold would be made in two or more parts. (For bisque and porcelain production, the molds are usually cast in plaster of Paris. Metal molds were also made from which to cast more plaster molds.)

Viscous porcelain slip is poured into the plaster molds from an opening in the bottom. The plaster mold absorbs some of the water from the slip and the remaining part retains a slightly firm shape when it is released from the mold. Then the cast portion is cleaned, smoothed and joined together if required so that the mold joining lines do not show. Additional features, such as an applied flower, may be added to the "green ware," and the finished figurine or doll is baked in a kiln at a very high temperature so that it will assume a hardened and permanent form. Then the figure is painted and decorated and the coloring is fired or "baked" into the piece. Mass-produced bisque or porcelain figures from the early years of the 20th century for the "better market" were given a "high firing," at a very high temperature. This produced a harder and smoother finish, but caused more loss in the firing process as some items would crack, bend or lose the proper shape. Most mass-produced porcelain and bisque figurines that are meant to sell for a low price today are given a "low firing." This causes less kiln loss but produces a product that is rougher to the touch and can fracture or break more easily if it is dropped or receives a blow from another object. A low firing also speeds up production. Most high-fired porcelain production for the mass market that was meant to sell at a reasonable price during the early years of the 20th century was completed in Germany, where labor costs were very low.

Germany was not formed as one nation until 1871 and it began to industrialize rapidly afterwards. Wages in Germany were low and workers were abundant. Adults and even young children labored in factories and also at home, providing components for factory finishing. Hundreds of porcelain-making factories had already been operating in the German states and they continued to fill the demand for merchandise made of porcelain, such as

Mona Nevins *Kewpie* collection when it was on display at Hobby City Doll & Toy Museum in Anaheim, California in the early 1990s. Note the rare *Kewpie* figurines on the middle section of shelves. *Courtesy of Mona Nevins.*

figurines and dolls for markets abroad. The United States had the largest middle class with more money to spend for children's toys than any other country in the world at the time, with the possible exception of Great Britain, which had a smaller population. The majority of the German porcelain factories were located in southern Germany in the historic region of Thuringia, around the towns of Sonneberg and Nuremberg. When Geo. Borgfeldt & Co. obtained the rights from Rose O'Neill to manufacture *Kewpie* in plastic mediums in 1912, the German firm Kestner & Comp, which produced high quality porcelain products at a low price, made most of them. The average cost of an all-bisque *Kewpie* doll or figurine before World War I was 15¢, which would be about $1.00 to $2.00 at today's values.

Another likely step in the production process is that a low-paid mold maker, who may have considered himself a designer, altered the samples sent to Germany by Borgfeldt and created additional sizes of a design or reworked them slightly to produce other variations of a figurine. It would be simple to change the arm positions of a seated *Kewpie* while it was still in the "soft" form and place it in various positions that would conform to a figurine that held a dog, a cat or another object. A seated *Kewpie* in the soft form could be changed slightly to ride a goose, a rocking horse or another animal. Nude dolls or figurines could have sculpted hats to create another character. Borgfeldt representatives who were located in Germany in the porcelain-producing towns could approve minor changes in production to make various products.

The purpose of *Kewpie* production on an extremely large scale would be to produce designs that could be quickly turned into figurines, made rapidly and immediately dispatched to the Borgfeldt company in New York. Borgfeldt would then sell them to other distributors and retailers so they could reach consumers as soon as possible. *Kewpie* was a "novelty item" and novelty items do not usually enjoy a long life of permanent production. Thousands of clever and original *Kewpie* novelty items have been produced since 1912. Unlike many other novelty pieces, these have withstood the test of time and have become permanent and classic images that are still available for retail sale.

Opposite page: The very rare "*Kewpie* Mountain," an exhibition model, *circa 1915. Image Courtesy of Theriault's, http://www.theriaults.com/.*

The Palmer Cox *Brownies*, another unique concept that went from illustrations to figurines and toys, were just as popular in the era right before *Kewpie* came along, but they did not have Joseph L. Kallus protecting and promoting them for seventy years. Kallus' marketing determination, now that of Jesco, has allowed *Kewpie* to endure to this day as high quality products.

Kewpie products in porcelain, bisque and china were made in hundreds of different forms and designs, both as figurines and as dolls. A great many of the thousands of samples that were made before World War I survive today, as they were always well thought of. The present value of *Kewpies* made in Germany before the United States entered World I (1917) is determined by several factors. The rare items are certainly worth more than the common ones. The common *Kewpie* products are usually simpler designs, showing a single figure in a standing position; the rare *Kewpies* are the larger ones or examples that show another figure with *Kewpie*, such as the *Kewpidoodle Dog* or a vase.

The Rose O'Neill *Kewpie* figurines shown here are sometimes considered "dolls" by people who do not realize that a *doll* by definition should have some moveable parts and should have originally been intended to be either a plaything for a child or made especially for a collector of children's toys. Many figurines of *Kewpie* are called "action figures" because they present *Kewpie* involved in some form of action. These porcelain *Kewpie* figures generally measure from 2-5in (5-13cm). Notable rarities are cited. These figurines were made in Germany from about 1912 to the 1920s, but importation to the United States was interrupted from about 1915 to 1919 because of World War I.

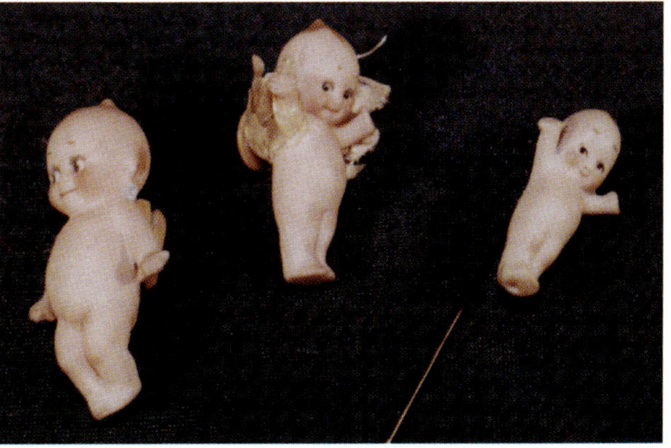

Three small novelties made in Germany. From left to right: Place card holder, 2½in (6cm); Buttonholer, 2in (5cm) and Stickpin, 1¾in (5cm). *Shirley Karaba Collection.*

***Kewpie* Action Figures**	
***Kewpie* Positions**	Baby with bottle (very rare)
	Two babies in a bunting
	One *Kewpie* feeding the other with a spoon from a porridge bowl
	Kewpie with hands in the air
	Seated and kicking out left leg
	Seated and kicking out right leg
	Lying on back with feet in the air
	Lying on stomach
	Polishing boot
	Wearing boots
	Wearing painted and fired "Mary Jane" shoes
	With molded clothing
	Peering out of a basket of flowers
***Kewpies* that are named because of their "action"**	Bather (with sand pail)
	Bookworm (seated with book on lap)
	Huggers (two *Kewpies* with arms wrapped around each other (The sizes are usually 3½in [9cm], 4in [10cm] and 5in [13cm])
	Indian (with molded clothing)
	Mother and Child (with large baby bottle)
	Readers (two *Kewpies* with an open book)
	Scholar (seated and holding a pen)
	Student (wearing glasses and reading a book)
	Thinker (One of the most common forms of *Kewpie* in all media. In porcelain, the sizes are from 3-6in [8-15cm], including each half-inch size.)
	Traveler (Carries an umbrella and a suitcase. Found in every size from 2-5in [5-13cm], including each half-inch size.)
	Traveler with *Kewpidoodle Dog* (much rarer than regular Traveler)
***Kewpie* Professions**	Aviator (with molded binoculars)
	Bellhop
	Boxer (a variation of the Huggers, but much rarer)
	Farmer
	Gardner
	Golfer
	Lawyer
	Governor (seated in a chair with crossed arms and legs)
	Mayor (seated in a wicker basket chair)
	Musician with a drum

***Kewpie* Professions** (continued)	Musician with a guitar
	Musician with a mandolin
	Policeman
	Soldier: Wearing a plumed helmet (very rare) German soldier coming out of an egg (very rare) Sitting soldier Wounded soldier Soldier wearing a Prussian helmet and dressed as a Prussian soldier Soldier wearing a "Rough Rider" hat American Confederate soldier
	Sweeper (with broom)
***Kewpie* with an Animal**	Bee on foot
	Butterfly in hand
	Cat on lap
	with two cats; one is black and one is gray
	with a chicken
	with a chicken coming out of an egg
	with a chicken and a vase full of eggs
	with *Kewpidoodle Dog*: *Kewpie* lying on his stomach and dog atop his back *Kewpie* and *Kewpidoodle Dog* on a log *Kewpie* seated on *Kewpidoodle Dog* *Kewpie* and *Kewpidoodle Dog* on a bench *Kewpie* and *Kewpidoodle Dog* on a bench; dog is being fed from a bottle *Kewpie* and *Kewpidoodle Dog* with an umbrella
	with an Elephant in two versions: Elephant on his back with *Kewpie* seated on his stomach Elephant is sitting alongside *Kewpie*
	Fly on *Kewpie*'s toe
	on a goose
	on a rocking horse
	on a dachshund
	on a dog
	on a rabbit
	on a goat
	on an elephant
	holding a teddy bear
	with a turkey

***Kewpie* with an Object**	Basket
	Basket on *Kewpie*'s back
	in bathtub
	in bed
	twins in a blanket (very rare)
	with buckets on a chain
	with yoke and buckets on a chain
	with a cup
	on a chair at a table set with a tea service
	with comb seated in bathtub
	with a hat and purse (attached to vase)
	holding a heart
	with a jack-o-lantern
	with knapsack
	with outhouse
	holding a pen
	with pen and inkwell
	with potted plant
	wrapped in a rose
	holding a rose
	holding a rose and seated in a hammock
	with flowers attached to a vase
	holding a sack
	seated in a sea shell
	standing on a sea shell
	with a shoe
	on a sled
	in a swing
	at a table
	on a tray (holding a pen)

Miscellaneous *Kewpie* Items of Bisque	
	Bottle top attached to a cork
	Boutonnière (attaches through a button hole)
	Buttons
	Place cards have 2-inch (5cm) *Kewpie* attached to a bisque holder: Reader Holding a Rose Mandolin Player Blunderboo
	Place Card that is a soldier shooting a bug
	Place Cards that attach to cups

Kewpidoodle Dog

- (Alone in sizes of 1½in [4cm], 3in [8cm], 4½in [12cm]; perhaps 5in [13cm])
- Attached to an olive green bisque box
- With a sunflower
- Molded to a bathtub

Jasperware Objects

- (Blue and white unless otherwise noted)
- Bank
- Covered tall bowl
- Flower bowl
- Finger bowl
- Sugar bowl
- Box ("Klothespin Box")
- Clock (also in green and pink)
- Wall plaques (also in green and pink)
- Plates
- Sugar and cream set
- Vases

China (glazed bisque) Objects

- Bank
- *Kewpie* lying on a box with a lid
- Child's tea set includes: teapot, sugar and creamer, plates, saucers, cups
- Child's Bavarian plate
- Baby dishes and baby feeding dishes
- Creamers
- Cups and saucers
- Inkwell
- Perfume bottles
- Pitcher
- Planter (with the Thinker)
- Plaques
- Talcum powder shakers
- Salt and pepper shakers
- Tray (some have matching coasters)

Bisque "Thinker," 4½in (12cm). Incised "O'Neill/Germany" on the bottom. *Shirley Karaba Collection.*

"Thinker" made of plaster, 4in (10cm). Incised "O'Neill/Germany" on the bottom. *Shirley Karaba Collection.*

Plaster black and white "Thinkers," 4in (10cm). Incised "O'Neill/Germany" on the bottom.

"Huggers," made in Germany, 3½in (9cm).

Right: "Huggers," 2¾in (7cm). From Japan, they are dressed in crepe paper as a bride and groom for a wedding cake topper. *Shirley Karaba Collection.*

Below: Genuine "Huggers," 3½in (9cm). The pair on the right are from Germany with a similar pair marked "Japan" on the left. (The cloth wreath in the girl's hair is an addition.) *Karen Shaker Collection.*

Seated action *Kewpie,* 3¼in (8cm). This figure is marked with the "KEWPIE" heart sticker and "©" on the bottom. *Shirley Karaba Collection.*

Kewpie with an attached basket, 2in (5cm). Marked with a "©" on the bottom. *Shirley Karaba Collection.*

Below: German-made *Kewpies*. "Bookworm" is 3½in (9cm); the other baby is 3½in (9cm) long. *Shirley Karaba Collection.*

Another view of Shirley Karaba's "Bookworm."

All-bisque "Action Kewpies" from Germany. Note the bugs on the two larger ones. *Courtesy of Theriault's, http://www.theriaults.com/.*

German place card *Kewpie* with a mandolin, 2 1/8in (5cm). Marked, "5514" on the bottom. *Shirley Karaba Collection.*

Genuine German *Kewpie* 3½-inch (9cm) "Sweeper" and 4¼-inch (11cm) celluloid doll, repainted for the White House Gift Shop in the 1920s. *Shirley Karaba Collection.*

Top to bottom:

Kewpie "Traveler," 3½in (9cm), is from Germany. *Karen Shaker Collection.*

Early German *Kewpies*, from left to right: "Readers," 3½in (9cm); "Traveler," 3¼in (8cm) and another "Traveler" with the *Kewpidoodle Dog*, 3¼in (8cm). All three are incised "O'Neill" on the bottom. The "Traveler" also has the 1913 copyright sticker on the back, as well as the heart decal on the front. *Shirley Karaba Collection.*

These three items—the "Travelers" on either side of a "Governor"—are imitations from Japan. Note the heart sticker on the one with the dog. It reads, "Kewpie // Made in Japan." Each is 2¼in (5cm). *Karen Shaker Collection.*

"Governor," 3½in (9cm). Sits in his chair. Marked "©" on the bottom. *Shirley Karaba Collection.*

"Policeman," 4½in (12cm). No markings, but nevertheless a genuine German *Kewpie.*

Below: A group of choice early Rose O'Neill *Kewpies* from Germany. *Courtesy of Theriault's, http://www.theriaults.com/.*

The German bisque *Kewpie* seated at a tea table is also known as "*Kewpie* at Breakfast." *Courtesy of Theriault's, http://www/theriaults.com/.*

This 4½-inch (12cm) *Kewpidoodle Dog* is one of the most fabulous and rare of all *Kewpie* collectibles. It is incised, "Rose O'Neill" and "©"on the bottom. The white mark on the *Kewpidoodle Dog's* head is a glare from the photographic lights. *Karen Shaker Collection.*

Karen Shaker's *Kewpidoodle Dog* with a 2¼-inch (6cm) item for size comparison.

Top right and left: Vase with attached *Kewpie*, 4¼in (11cm). Note the dogs on either side of the vase. The bottom is incised "AK 627" and is also incised with the J.D. Kestner crown symbol.

Vase, 5¼in (13cm). Incised with the Goebel crown mark and "WG" on the bottom. *Shirley Karaba Collection.*

The following are considered to be *Kewpies* by collectors, but they are actually knock-offs or imitations from Asia. This practice of imitating a popular commercial item has always existed. Although it is illegal, it is difficult to police and the pieces sell because they are usually much cheaper than a genuine *Kewpie*, or whatever popular item they capitalize on without paying royalties. These bogus collectibles sometimes have a high value to collectors if they are well made. This is particularly true of the *Kewpie* "Policeman" and "Indian," which are even incised "Rose O'Neill."

Left: "Made in Occupied Japan" figure holding a "Kewpie doll," 3¾in (10cm).

Left, bottom: Another version of the "Made in Occupied Japan" china figurine holding a famous doll, 3¾in (10cm). *Karen Shaker Collection.*

Kewpie holding a pot, 5¼in (13cm). This figurine is marked "4541." on the back and is probably a knock-off from Japan. *Shirley Karaba Collection.*

Three Lefton *Kewpie* knock-offs made in Japan during the 1970s. They are marked "KW 228" on the bottom and are about 3½-4½in (9-12cm) tall. All Lefton Kewpie-type figurines are unauthorized, or pirated designs. Collectors like to augment genuine collections with look-alike things. *Bette Ann Axe Collection.*

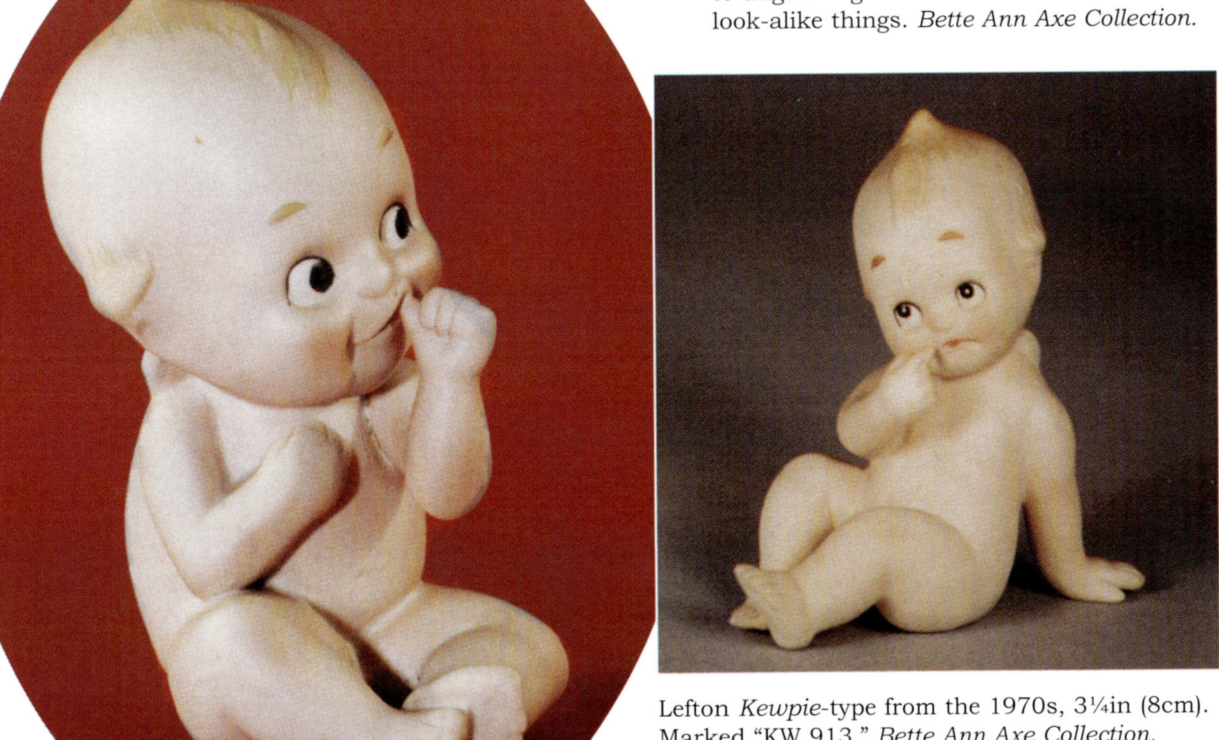

Lefton *Kewpie*-type from the 1970s, 3¼in (8cm). Marked "KW 913." *Bette Ann Axe Collection.*

Left: Lefton *Kewpie* knock-off, 5in (13cm). From Japan in the 1970s,

Lefton vase, 7¼in (19cm). Marked "KW 336" on the bottom. *Shirley Karaba Collection.*

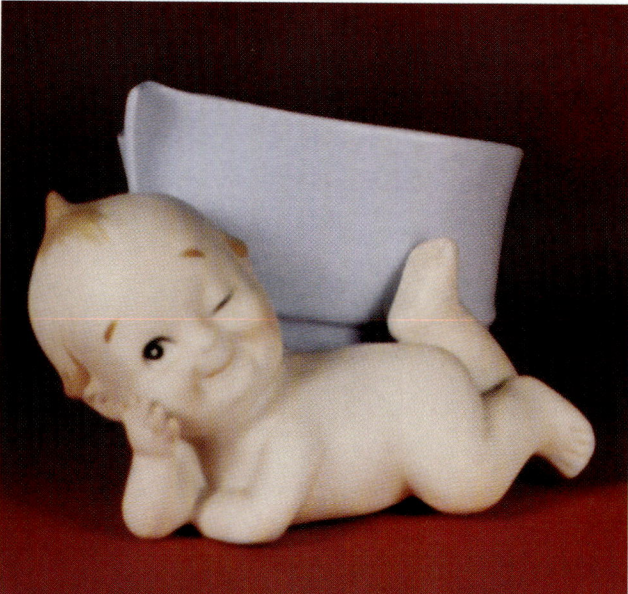

Lefton vase, 2½in (6cm). Stamped "KW 275" on the bottom. *Karen Shaker Collection.*

Below: Lefton figurines that resemble *Kewpie,* 2½in (6cm) and 3¼in (8cm). These were made in Taiwan, probably during the 1980s and they are stamped "3175" on the bottom. *Karen Shaker Collection.*

Lefton "professions," 3in (9cm). A set of figurines made in Taiwan in 1985. Again, they look too much like *Kewpies* for it to be a coincidence. *Karen Shaker Collection.*

Three more Lefton "professions" made in Taiwan in 1985 that are variances on the above group.

Kewpie-type figurine from Japan, 3in (9cm). Probably from the 1970s.

Candy dish, 5in (13cm). Made in Japan by Norcrest, another company that did knock-offs on *Kewpie. Karen Shaker Collection.*

Kewpie-type with a dog, 2¼in (6cm). No marks.

Kewpie figurines, 6in (15cm). These are quality products, but are still likely to be imitations, although they are incised "Kewpie // Rose O'Neill // ©" on the back. They are finished with shiny, glazed costumes and a matte effect on the body sections. A sticker on the bottoms of each item reads: "ORIGINAL ARN ART // CREATION // JAPAN." *Karen Shaker Collection.*

Left: Another "Policeman," 6in (15cm). Marked "O'Neill" like the one from the Karen Shaker Collection. On the bottom he is also stamped: "7863" with a crossed arrows logo.

Reproductions of *Kewpidoodle Dog* in sizes 1½ - 2½in (4 - 6cm).

Right: Commercially made china *Kewpie* knock-offs, purchased in gift shops in the 1980s. The *Kewpidoodle Dog* is 2¼in (6cm) tall.

There are many, many genuine *Kewpie* collectibles in all sorts of forms, as a wide variety of *Kewpie* merchandise has been available since 1912. The chinaware and silver products are especially collectible and costly now. They were not economical when they were new during the 1910s and therefore are rather scarce today.

Glass candy containers, 3¼in (8cm). The one on the right is painted. It is not known if this is factory-original condition. Each one is embossed "SERIAL NO. 2862" on the bottom of *Kewpie* portion of the piece. On the bottom of the candy dish side they are embossed "GEO. BORGFELDT & CO., N.Y. // KEWPIE // REG.U.S.PAT. OFF. // DES. PAT. 43680." *Shirley Karaba Collection.*

Sterling silver spoon that says "KEWPIE" on the handle, 5in (13cm). It is also marked "©" and cites the manufacturer, the Paye & Baker Mfg. Co. of North Attleboro, Massachusetts. It probably dates from the early 1900s. *Donna Felger Collection.*

Child's dishes by Royal Rudolstadt. Marked "Copyrighted Rose O'Neill Wilson // Kewpie Germany." *Shirley Karaba Collection.*

Royal Rudolstadt child's cup.

China cup and matching saucer by Z.S. & Co., Bavaria. Marked "Copyrighted // Mrs. Rose O'Neil [sic] Wilson." *Shirley Karaba Collection.*

Child size cup by Z.S. & Co., Bavaria. *Shirley Karaba Collection.*

Shallow baby's dish marked "Kewpie // Copyright by // Rose O'Neill Wilson" *Shirley Karaba Collection.*

Left: Child's dish, 5¼in (13cm). Marked "M.Z. Austria." This is probably not a genuine *Kewpie* article. *Shirley Karaba Collection.*

China salt shaker, 2½in (6cm). Has the 1913 Rose O'Neill copyright label. *Shirley Karaba Collection.*

Green Jasperware Pitcher. The bottom is incised "Rose O'Neill // Kewpie // Germany." *Shirley Karaba Collection.*

Pink Jasperware-type plaque with no marks. It says "THE KUTIES" on the front. That tells the story. *Shirley Karaba Collection.*

Pink and green *Kewpie* plaques made of porcelain, 7in (18cm). From 1973. They are © World Wide Arts, Inc., Cleveland, Ohio and are made in Japan. Incised "© Jos. L. Kallus // MCMLXXIII." *Karen Shaker Collection.*

Pink *Kewpie* plaque by World Wide Arts, Inc., 7in (18cm). From 1973. Marked like the others. *Karen Shaker Collection.*

Collector's china plate, 10½in (27cm) in diameter. From 1973. Part of a series. Produced by World Wide Arts, Inc. of Cleveland, Ohio. Made in Japan. Marked "© Jos. L. Kallus // MCMLXXIII. *Shirley Karaba Collection.*

Below: *Kewpie* soaps, 4-5in (10-13cm) tall. Produced in the early 20th century. The smaller one is embossed on the back: "KEWPIE // MADE IN USA //PAT PEND // US DES UPF (?)" and "433 (?)." *Shirley Karaba Collection.*

Above: This is probably not an authorized *Kewpie* item, but it is from the early *Kewpie* years. The wording at the top is "KEWPIES // Q.P.S. A COMPOUND // FOR COLDS." It cost 50¢ a box. *Shirley Karaba Collection.*

Heavy brass *Kewpie* figurine, 4in (10cm). It may have had some utilitarian use originally, such as a car hood ornament. Silver charm, 7/8in (2cm) tall. This charm is marked "KEWPIE" on the front and "O'NEILL" on the back. At the right is a pewter napkin holder or calling card holder, 1 1/8in (3cm) tall. All three of these *Kewpie* articles are early 20th century in origin.

Silver saltshaker, 3in (8cm) tall. It is marked with three indecipherable letters in a circle and "TRADE // KEWPIE // MARK." It probably dates from the 1910s.

Below: All of these tiny items have the *Kewpie* image on them. Note the lady's thimble for size relations. The silver ring at the far right is meant for a baby. The bracelet with ten ivory Kewpies on it is probably not an authorized *Kewpie* piece. The item to the right of the spoon with an enameled bowl is a whistle. All except the spoon with the enamel bowl are early collectibles. *Shirley Karaba Collection.*

Sterling silver spoon with an enameled bowl, a souvenir of Bonniebrook. On the bowl it says, "ROSE O'NEILL 1874-1944. *Shirley Karaba Collection.*

Below left: One-piece Talcum shaker, $6\frac{7}{8}$in (17cm). Made of composition, 1910s. *Shirley Karaba Collection.*

Below right: Side view of the composition *Kewpie* talcum shaker, showing the metal plug with holes for the powder to be dispensed. *Shirley Karaba Colleciton.*

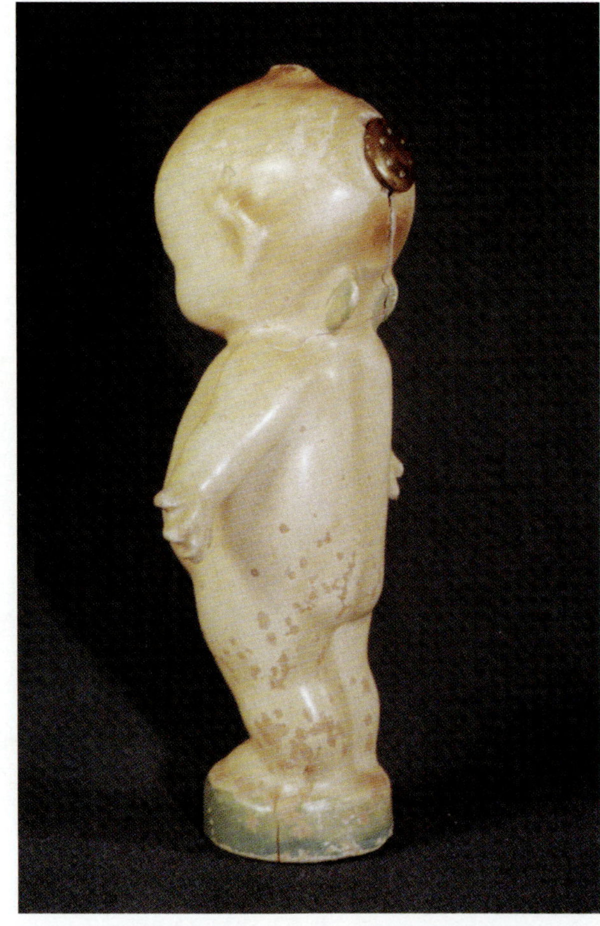

Two of the fifteen *Kewpie* "flannels" that were a premium with tobacco. They were supposed to be sewn together to form a pillow top. In the lower right corner "ROSE O'NEILL" and "© 1914" are printed. *Karen Shaker Collection.*

Vintage framed, hand-tinted print, 6in x 19½in (15cm x 50cm). It shows several *Kewpie* dolls and figurines, circa 1915. The dog at the left in the picture has nothing to do with *Kewpies*. This same print has been seen in the identical frame in other collections. It must have been some sort of premium when it was new. *Karen Shaker Collection.*

Some of the unauthorized *Kewpie* merchandise is at least unique or innovative in design. Several banks, vases and other utilitarian pieces have been made over the years. Some of them are not very accurate copies of the *Kewpie* image, but there is no mistaking their original intent. All the ones shown here were produced by commercial enterprises.

Porcelain salt and pepper shakers, 3½in (9cm). Note the little blue *Kewpie* wings on this set. They are each stamped on the bottom: "© INARCO // 1961 // E-184."

Below: Two different sets of *Kewpie*-inspired salt and pepper shakers. They are from the 1960s/1970s. *Karen Shaker Collection.*

Vase, 6in (15cm). This vase has wonderful modeling. It is probably from the 1970s. No markings. *Karen Shaker Collection.*

Below: Plain light blue vase, 5½in (14cm) tall. No markings. These come in many sizes and colors. *Karen Shaker Collection.*

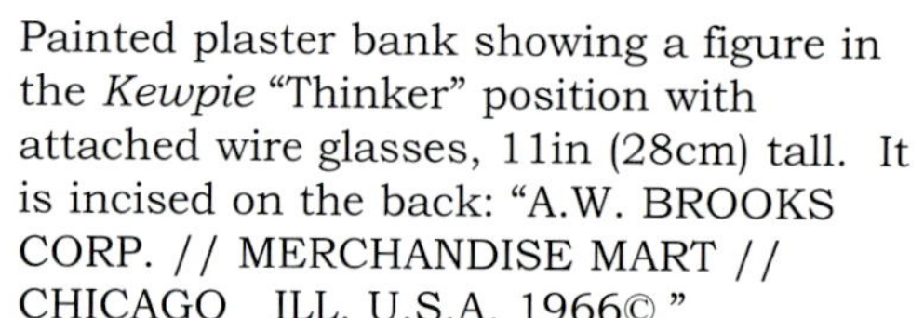

Painted plaster bank showing a figure in the *Kewpie* "Thinker" position with attached wire glasses, 11in (28cm) tall. It is incised on the back: "A.W. BROOKS CORP. // MERCHANDISE MART // CHICAGO ILL. U.S.A. 1966©."

Painted vinyl bank, 9in (23cm). Note the red heart on the chest and the little wings at the shoulders. It is marked: "© 1977 A.BEE SYNDICATE, INC. // MADE IN HONG KONG."

Chapter 3

Dolls

Kewpie will always be the most famous doll associated with Rose O'Neill. *Kewpie* dolls came from the magazine illustrations that Miss O'Neill first created in 1909. After 1912, dolls were produced from the models that Joseph L. Kallus made. The earliest dolls were made in Germany and they had jointed arms only. These bisque German dolls came in many different sizes, from about 2-13in (5-33cm). They were also made of celluloid. Some of the early dolls were produced in such abundance that molds that were used over and over and copied and recopied, resulted in many size variations. The most common doll sizes are given in the accompanying charts.

Rose O'Neill created *Scootles* in 1925. She may have done the original sculpting, as a famous photograph shows, but Kallus changed and refined the design over the years. In late 1940, Rose O'Neill developed *Ho-Ho*, "the Little Laughing Buddha," which was more a figurine than a doll, as it had no moving parts, and Kallus later refined and changed this design when he marketed *Ho-Ho* in vinyl in the 1960s. This later doll caused controversy when it was released, as many people of the Buddhist religion were offended by the representation of the founder of their faith used as an image for children's toys.

When Joseph Kallus founded the Rex Doll Co. in 1916 one of the leading products of the company was the composition *Kewpie* with jointed arms distributed by the Tip Top Toy Co. for use as carnival prizes. The enormous popularity of these dolls is still evident, as people who know nothing about dolls refer to "Carnival *Kewpie* Dolls." Mr. Kallus also developed many dolls of his own design, such as *Baby Bundie* in 1918 and *Miss Peep* in 1960, and dolls of licensed figures, such as *Felix the Cat, Pinocchio* and *Betty Boop.*

There are two other dolls that are considered part of the *Kewpie* family. These are *Giggles*, a composition doll of the late 1940s that was packaged in the same boxes as *Kewpie* at the time. The boxes carried *Kewpie* logos and pictures of *Kewpie. Giggles* is a Joseph L. Kallus design. The other doll of the *Kewpie* family is *Kewpie Gal.* This one is actually a *Kewpie* with molded hair in a page-boy style, making it clearly represent a girl.

Kewpie

Bisque		
1912+ Made in Germany by Kestner, Gebr.Voigt, Herman Voigt, Hertwig & Co., and others. Made in U.SA. by Fulper Pottery.	1. All-bisque with jointed arms only.	
	2in (5cm)	7½in (19cm)
	2½in (6cm)	8in (20cm)
	4in (10cm)	9in (23cm)
	4½in (12cm)	10½in (27cm)
	5in (13cm)	11in (28cm)
	6in (15cm)	12in (31cm)
	7in (18cm)	13in (33cm)
	2. All-bisque with jointed arms and legs.	
	4in (10cm)	
	5½in (14cm)	
	3. Bisque shoulder head; arms; legs. Cloth body. Painted eyes.	
	6in (15cm)	
	12in (31cm)	
	4. Bisque head; flange neck; composition body; round glass eyes.	
	13½in (34cm)	

This Kewpie Doll

Premium No. 6011

Given for Four Subs‹ riptions

THE ‹rresistible little Kewpies have taken the ‹ountry by storm. Their quaint contageous smile and roguish appearance win an instantaneous reception in the hearts of both little folks and grownups. Kewpie says: "Folks say I don't have to make friends: that I just naturally am friends anyhow." These dolls that **Needlecraft** offers her friends are colored in natural flesh-tints and stand full six inches high. The bodies and faces are carefully molded and the arms are pivoted, so they may be placed in many laughable positions. They are washable.

Let us send you a joy - bringing, mirth - provoking Kewpie. We assure you that once you see the little dear you will feel the same Kewpish love as Rose O'Neil did when she wrote:

"From Kewpie you'll not wish to part,
But when you've learned his smile by heart,
Just give that little smile away
To everybody, every day."

SPECIAL OFFER If you will send us a club of four subscriptions to Needlecraft at our regular subscription-price of 25 cents each, we will send each subscriber this paper for one year, and we will send you a Kewpie Doll (Premium No. 6011), all charges prepaid.

NEEDLECRAFT, Augusta, Maine

Advertisement for a Kewpie doll used as a premium for selling subscriptions to *Needlecraft*, 1914.

All-bisque *Kewpie* doll with jointed arms, 9½in (24cm). Circa 1912. These dolls usually have "O'NEILL" and various numbers incised on the bottom of the feet. The red banded with gold sticker on the chest says, "KEWPIE // Germany." A small, round sticker on the back of this one reads, "DESIGN PATENTED." These little round stickers can also say, "Copyright 1913." Note the little blue wings at *Kewpie's* neck, a feature found on most bisque dolls and figurines.

Left: Bisque *Kewpie* dolls, 5¼in (13cm), 5½in (14cm) and 5¾in (15cm). Note that the one on the right with the heart sticker has sharper modeling and more details in the hair. The bisque is also smoother in finish.

All-bisque dolls, 4¼in (11cm), 5½in (14cm) and 6¼in (16cm). Note the slight variations in hair painting from other similar dolls. The lace bonnet on the center doll may be original. *Karen Shaker Collection.*

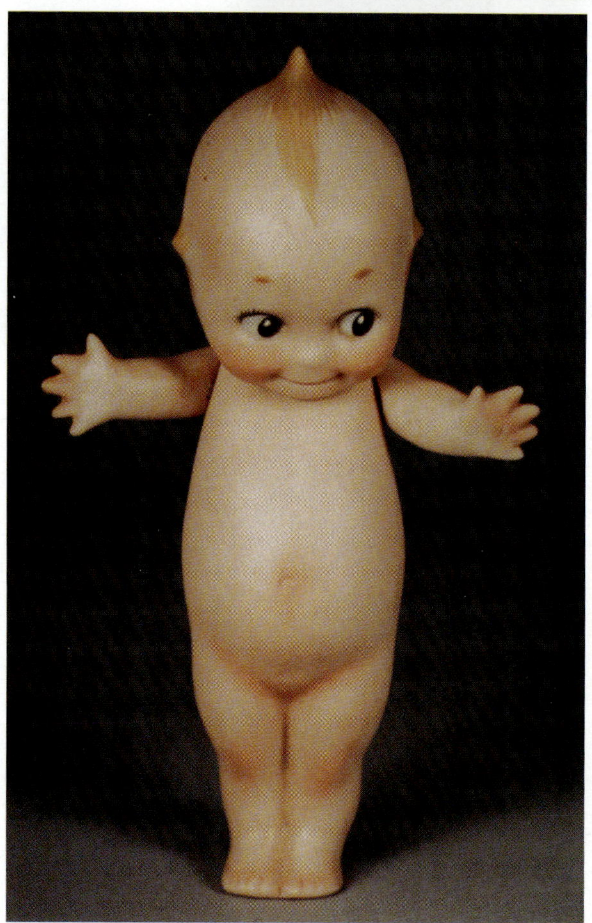

All-bisque doll, 6½in (17cm). *Bette Ann Axe Collection.*

Bisque doll with jointed arms from a series with felt clothing, 4½in (12cm). Circa 1917-1918. Note the painted shoes. He has the "1913" label. *Shirley Karaba Collection.*

Original box for 4½-inch (12cm) dressed doll. *Shirley Karaba Collection.*

Below: All-original dressed dolls with painted shoes, 4½in (12cm). Circa 1917-1918. Note the hats and the original boxes. *Shirley Karaba Collection.*

All-bisque dressed "Bride" with jointed arms, 4½in (12cm). Marked "NIPPON." Even if the clothing is not original, it is certainly vintage. *Karen Shaker Collection.*

Below: *Kewpie* figurines, Jasperware items and the fabulous JD. Kestner doll with a bisque head and composition body. The eyes are glass. The doll is from the 1910s and is about 13½in (34cm) tall. *Courtesy of Theriault's, http://www.theriaults.com/.*

This 10-inch (25cm) doll was given as the Banquet Souvenir of a United Federation of Doll Clubs, Inc. regional convention in March of 1980 in San Francisco, California. The head with molded bunny ears is bisque; the body is stuffed cloth.

Below: Glass-eyed *Kewpie* by Kestner, 13½in (33cm). Circa 1914, with a bisque head and a jointed composition body. The doll-size tea servicc is from Germany. *Courtesy of Theriault's, http://www.theriaults.com/.*

Celluloid

1915+

Made in Germany by Karl Standfuss. Made in Japan by various firms.

Most have jointed arms.

2in (5cm)	5¼in (13cm)
2¼in (6cm)	6½in (17cm)
2½in (6cm)	7in (18cm)
3in (8cm)	7½in (19cm)
3¼in (8cm)	8in (20cm)
3½in (9cm)	10in (25cm)
4in (10cm)	11¼in (28cm)
4½in (12cm)	22in (56cm)
5in (13cm)	

The 2¼—2½in (6cm) sizes also comes in a black version, referred to as a *Hottentot.*

There are also many novelty *Kewpies* in celluloid with no jointed parts:

3in (8cm) with a rabbit
3in (8cm) Instructor
3in (8cm) (and other sizes) Bride and Groom wedding cake decoration
3½in (9cm) Huggers
4in (10cm) Bather with a painted suit

There are many *Kewpie* knock-offs from Japan, such as a two-sided doll that is a *Billikin* on one side and a *Kewpie* on the other. Some of the Japanese unlicensed *Kewpies* with jointed arms look just like a genuine *Kewpie*; others resemble *Kewpie*, more or less.

Celluloid "Patriotic *Kewpies*" with jointed arms, 2¼in (6cm). These are German imports but are dressed in American World War I themes. The one on the left is attached to a candy box. *Shirley Karaba Collection.*

German celluloid doll with jointed arms, 5¼in (13cm). The back is marked "3/O."

Right: German celluloid dolls, 22in (56cm) and 10in (25cm). The smaller one is marked, "5." *Shirley Karaba Collection.*

German-made "Bride and Groom" *Kewpie* dolls with crepe paper clothing, 3in (8cm). These were used as wedding cake toppers or as favors. The backs are marked "8/0."

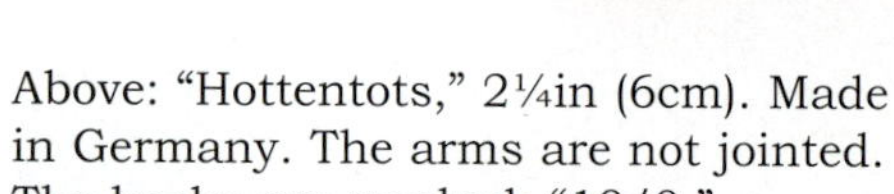

Above: "Hottentots," 2¼in (6cm). Made in Germany. The arms are not jointed. The backs are marked: "10/0."

"Hottentot" with arms extended upward, 2¼in (6cm). The white version has the arms in the usual position for a non-jointed celluloid doll of this size. Made in Germany. *Karen Shaker Collection.*

Celluloid doll with a crepe paper hat, 4in (10cm). No markings. *Karen Shaker Collection.*

Celluloid dolls with jointed arms and legs that resemble "Ragsy *Kewpie*," 3¾in (10cm) and 5¾in (15cm) tall. They are both marked "MADE IN JAPAN" and are not authentic *Kewpies. Shirley Karaba Collection.*

Above: Boy and girl with a *Kewpie*-type doll, 4¼in (11cm). No markings, but probably from Japan in the 1920s. *Bette Ann Axe Collection.*

Above right: *Kewpie* knock-offs, 2½in (6cm) and 3in (8cm). Marked "JAPAN." They have jointed arms.

Celluloid "Bride and Groom" *Kewpie*-types, 5½in (14cm). Marked "MADE IN JAPAN." Crepe paper clothing. *Shirley Karaba Collection.*

Composition 1916+ Made in U.S.A. by Joseph L. Kallus for **Rex Doll Co.**, **Mutual Doll Co.**, **Cameo Doll Co.**, **Noma Electric Corporation (Effanbee Dolls)**, and **Effanbee Doll Corporation.**	1. With jointed arms; usually attached to a base of "pedestal;" can have mohair wigs over molded hair (early years). 7in (18cm) 8-8½in (20-22cm) 10in (25cm) 11½in (29cm) 12-12½in (31-32cm) 2. With jointed arms; free-standing with legs apart; also as a black doll (1940s) 11½in (29cm) 3. Fully-jointed (1940s) 8in (20cm) 11in (28cm) 12in (31cm) 13in (33cm) 15in (38cm) 4. Composition head; cloth body 12in (31cm) 23in (58cm) Note: In 1923, an all-composition *Kewpie* sold for 58¢ in the 8-inch (20cm) size; in the late 1940s, the fully-jointed composition *Kewpie* from Noma Electric (Effanbee) was $2.00.
Dollmasters/ Theriaults 2002+	12in (31cm) (reproduction made in Germany by Ino Schaller—the material is called papier mâché.)

Early composition *Kewpie* with jointed arms, 7in (18cm). This example has the red heart sticker on the chest and the "© 1913" label on the back.

Composition *Kewpie* with jointed arms, 8½in (22cm). This one has the chest label and the "1913" label on the bottom of the feet. Note that the molding is sharper and the painting better than other examples. *Shirley Karaba Collection.*

Above: Composition dolls with jointed arms used as Talcum powder shakers, 7in (18cm). The bride's dress has disintegrated beyond repair. The heart sticker reads: "KEWPIE // TALCUM // Reg. U.S. // Pat. Off." *Karen Shaker Collection.*

Close-up of "Talcum Powder Bride." This is a good example of the early composition *Kewpie* doll with jointed arms only. These may have been made in one of the first Kallus factories. *Karen Shaker Collection.*

Early composition doll with jointed arms, 12½in (32cm). Many of the early "Carnival *Kewpies*" were molded to a base like this one.

Below: Close-up of the "Carnival *Kewpie*." The heart sticker reads: "KEWPIE // DESIGN PAT. // NO. 43680 // REG. U.S. // PAT. OFF." This one has especially nice coloring and painting and also has blue wings. Probably dates from before 1920.

Another variation of the "Carnival *Kewpie*" with jointed arms, 12½in (32cm). *Shirley Karaba Collection.*

Below: Black version of the "Carnival *Kewpie*" with jointed arms, 12½in (32cm). Like the others, it probably dates from before 1920. *Shirley Karaba Collection.*

Left: Composition *Kewpie* with jointed arms only, 11½in (29cm). This is probably from Effanbee, circa 1946. Note the excellent coloring and modeling.

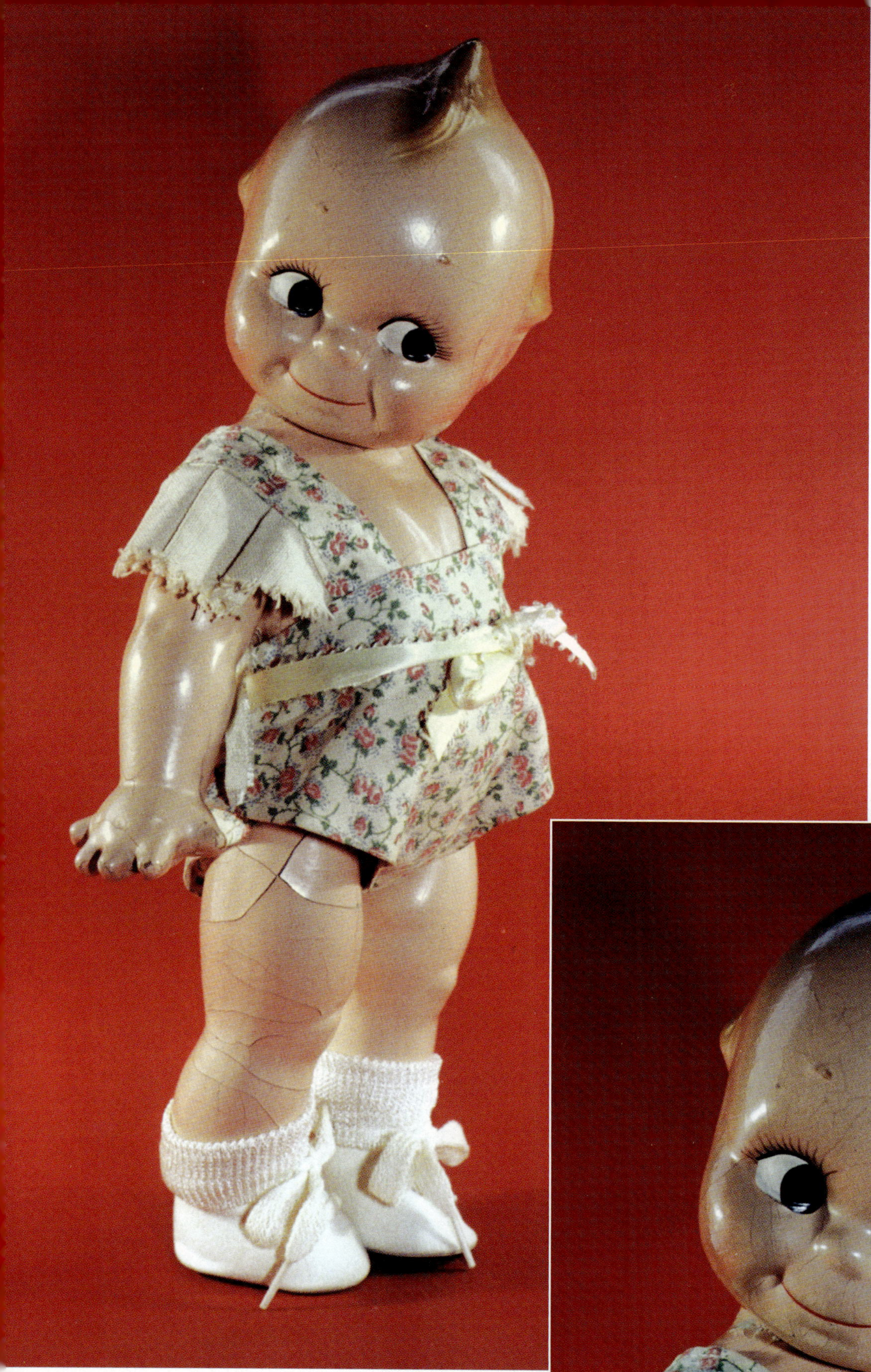

Fully-jointed *Kewpie* in the original sun suit, 13in (33cm). By Effanbee, circa 1946.

Close-up of fully-jointed Effanbee, circa 1946.

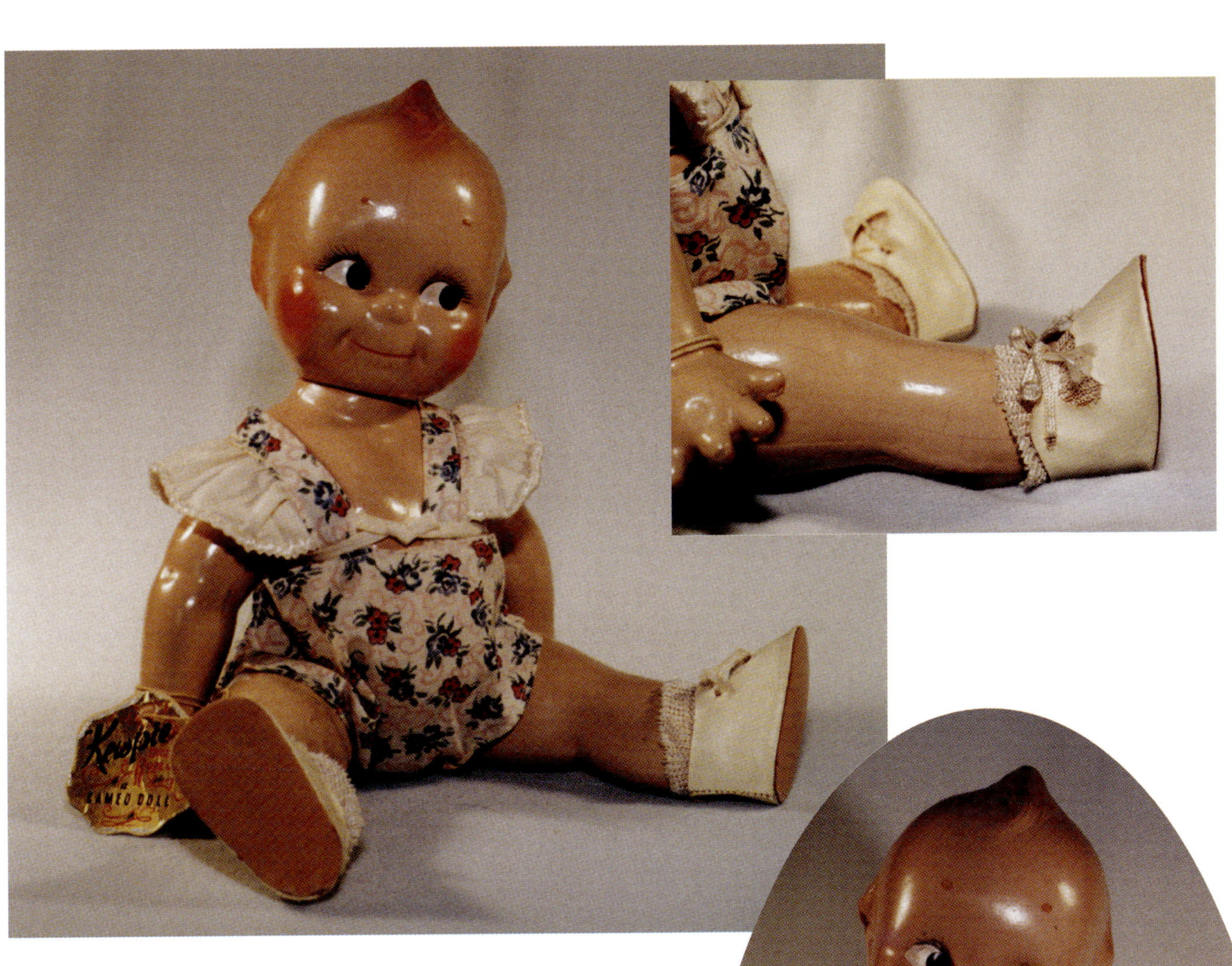

Fully-jointed, all-original composition doll, 13in (33cm). Distributed by Effanbee with a Cameo hang tag, circa 1946. *Shirley Karaba Collection.*

Inset: Close-up of Shirley Karaba's 13-inch (33cm) doll showing the original shoes that these *Kewpies* wore. Note also the typical "starfish" *Kewpie* hands.

All-composition, fully-jointed doll, 13in (33cm). From the Effanbee period in an original jersey bathing suit. *Shirley Karaba Collection.*

Cloth	
	Richard G. Kreuger, Inc. *Kewpies* made of all-cloth with a mask face and a jersey body in red, blue, green, coral, yellow, and pink.
1926+	8in (20cm)
Made in U.S.A. after 1926 by **King Innovations, Inc**. Made in U.SA. after 1936 by **Richard G.. Kreuger, Inc.**	11in (28cm)
	14in (36cm)
	17in (43cm)
	21in (53cm)
	King Innovations, Inc. *Kewpies* made with a mask face and a plush body:
	9in (23cm)
	12in (31cm)
	15in (38cm)
	18in (46cm)
	22in (56cm)
	King Innovations *Kewpies* in all-cloth wearing dresses:
	10in (25cm)
1999+	**R. John Wright Dolls, Inc.**
	2¼in (6cm) (lapel pin)
	6½in (17cm) (fully-jointed felt doll w/ felt clothing; many different characters, including black *Hottentot*
	8in (20cm) fully-jointed felt *Klassic Kewpie* and *Millennium Kewpie*
2000	**Dakin**
	4½in (12cm) boxed finger puppet

Kreuger cloth *Kewpie* with an "O'Neill" tag, 11in (28cm). *Shirley Karaba Collection.*

Right: Kreuger *Kewpie,* 8in (20cm). The tag is missing. *Karen Shaker Collection.*

Opposite page: All-cloth *Kewpies* with painted mask-faces from the 1930s. The smaller on is 10in (25cm) tall and was made by King Innovations, Inc. The larger one is 17in (43cm) tall and was made by Richard G. Kreuger, Inc. *Wanda Lodwick Collection.*

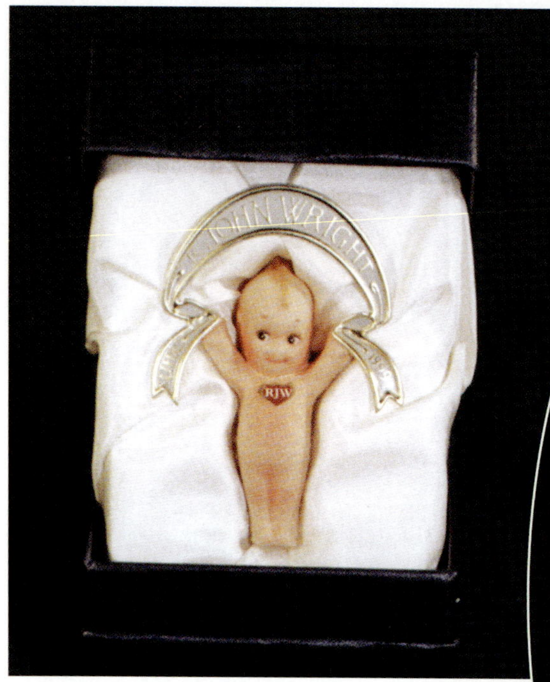

R. John Wright felt *Kewpie* lapel pin, 2¼in (6cm). Copyright 1999. This was a souvenir of a luncheon at the United Federation of Doll Clubs Convention in Washington, D.C. *Shirley Karaba Collection.*

Right: *Fleur*, 6½in (17cm). This was an edition of 250 fully-jointed felt dolls made for the UFDC Convention in Washington, D.C., 1999. *Shirley Karaba Collection.*

Little Mermaid Finger Puppet, 4½in (12cm). Dakin's version of a "Mer-Kewp." Made in China in 2000. *Karen Shaker Collection.*

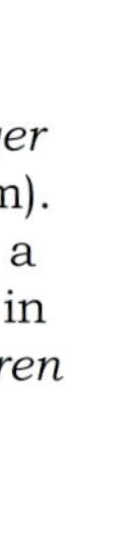

Hard Plastic	**Noma Electric Corporation/Effanbee Doll Company**
1949	13½in (34cm) (all-hard plastic, fully-jointed *Kewpie* with sleep eyes from Effanbee)
Early 1950s	9in (23cm) (jointed arms; perhaps made by Effanbee)
1986	**Jesco Imports, Inc.**
	6½in (17cm) (jointed arms; has a hole in the topknot of hair for a ribbon or with a plain topknot)

Hard Plastic *Kewpie,* 9in (23cm). From the 1950s or 1960s, possibly made by Cameo. Jointed arms only. Marked with a *Kewpie* sticker on the chest and on the back: "KEWPIE © BY ROSE O'NEILL."

Jesco *Kewpie,* 6½in (17cm). From 1986, this doll has a solid front package that opens like a door with the doll behind a window. Jointed arms; there is a hole in the hair for a bow. Marked on back: "JESCO TM © 1986 // MADE IN HONG KONG."

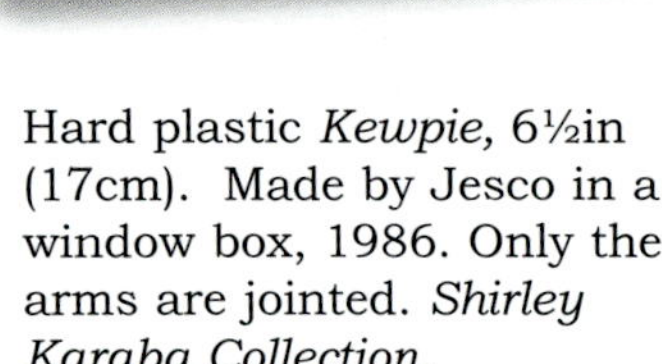
Hard plastic *Kewpie,* 6½in (17cm). Made by Jesco in a window box, 1986. Only the arms are jointed. *Shirley Karaba Collection.*

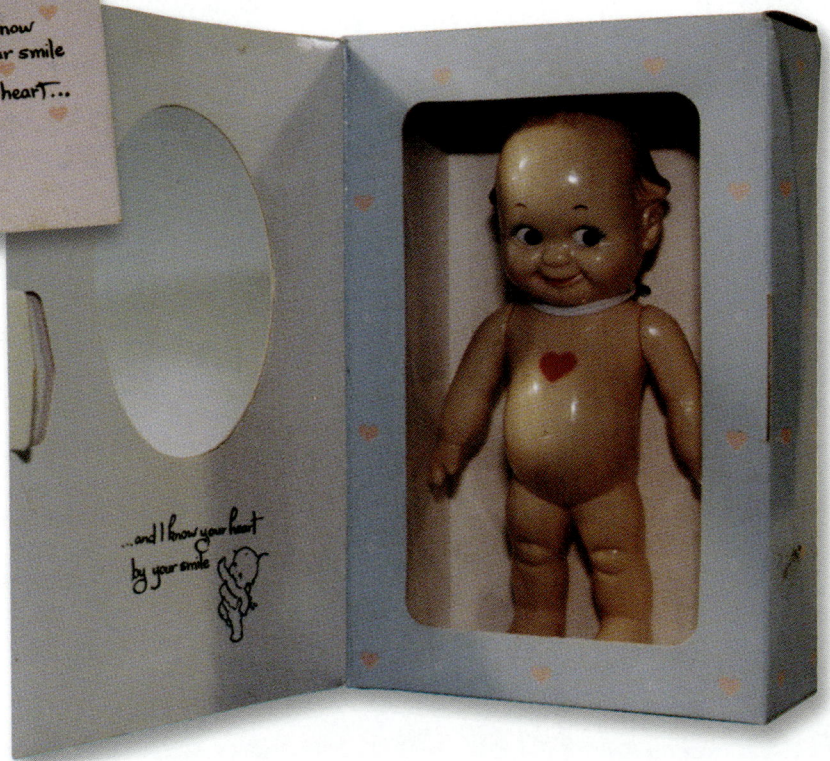

Vinyl

From circa 1952 to the present

Cameo Doll Products, 1952-1968; **Strombecker Corp.**, 1969-1972; **Knickerbocker**, 1972-1973; **Milton Bradley (Amsco)**, 1973-1976.

All these vinyl dolls cited Cameo Doll Products in some way. Some had a hang tag and some had a sticker or printed matter on the packaging with "Cameo" credited. Most of these vinyl dolls are marked: "CAMEO // ©." Some also have the initials "J.L.K." Some have heads marked "1965 // J.L.K."

Sizes of vinyl dolls:

1. With inset plastic eyes
   - 9½-11in (24-28cm)

2. Vinyl head and arms; blow mold body and legs (thin plastic)
   - 13½in (34cm)
   - 19½ (50cm)
   - 27in (69cm)

3. With rooted hair
   - 13in (33cm)
   - 21in (53cm)

4. Thinker (one-piece)
   - 3½-4in (9-10cm)

5. *Ragsy Kewpie*; jointed head only; one-piece body
   - 7½-11in (19-28cm)

6. All-vinyl; jointed head only
   - 4¼in (11cm)
   - 6-6½in (15-17cm)
   - 9-13in (23-33cm)

7. All-vinyl; fully-jointed
   - 7½-8½in (19-22cm)
   - 11in (28cm)
   - 14in (36cm)
   - 15in (38cm)
   - 16in (41cm)

8. Vinyl/cloth; some bodies are a combination of plush and cloth; some have bunny ears
   - 7-9in (18-23cm)
   - 12-18in (31-46cm)

Vinyl (continued)	All-vinyl *Kewpies* since 1983:
1983-1995	**Jesco**
	8in (20cm)
	12in (31cm)
	16in (41cm)
	21in (53cm) (baby with vinyl head, cloth body)
	25in (64cm)
1993-1994 (Made in China)	**Rose Art**
	7½in (19cm)
	9in (23cm)
	17in (43cm) (baby)
1997	**Lee Middleton Original Dolls, Inc.**
	12in (31cm)
	16in (41cm)
1999-2002 (Made in China)	**Effanbee Doll Company**
	8in (20cm)
	12in (31cm)
	16in (41cm)
1999-2000	**Goldberger Doll Company**
	4in (10cm)
	7½in (19cm)
	12in (31cm) (baby with vinyl head; cloth body)
2003+	**Cameo Collectibles**
	8in (20cm)
	12in (31cm)
	16in (41cm)
	16in (41cm) (baby with vinyl head; cloth body)

Fully-jointed Cameo *Kuddly Kewpie,* 13in (33cm). From 1966 with the original box. *Shirley Karaba Collection.*

Fully-jointed Cameo *Kewpie,* 11in (28cm). From the 1960s. *Shirley Karaba Collection.*

Opposite page: Three Cameo *Kewpies* from the 1960s. All are re-dressed. The tallest one is fully-jointed; the others have only jointed heads. The sizes are 13½in (34cm), 10in (25cm) and 6½in (17cm).

Cameo dolls, 7½in (9cm). Fully-jointed so-called "Katie O'Kewp" with a wreath on her head with one that has only a jointed head. *Karen Shaker Collection.*

Above: Cameo with a jointed head and plastic sleep eyes, 11in (28cm). *Karen Shaker Collection.*

Left: Vinyl "Thinker," 3½in (9cm) with two jointed-head *Kewpies* wearing their original red pants, 4½in (12cm). All are incised "O'NEILL" and "Cameo."

Redressed Cameo *Kewpie,* 19½in (50cm). This doll has a vinyl head and arms and plastic blow-mold body and legs.

Cameo *Kewpie,* 13½in (34cm).

Kuddly Kewpie baby in its original box, 18in (46cm). By Cameo. Jointed head; hinge-jointed arms and legs. *Shirley Karaba Collection.*

In the late 1960s-early 1970s Strombecker produced a series of *Kewpies* in their pajamas boxed like this one with a shrink-wrap front for the package. Only the heads are jointed. This is No. 6181 and it is 10½in (27cm) tall. The original price was $3.44. *Karen Shaker Collection.*

Below: Two Strombeckers in pajamas, 10½in (27cm). (The black one may be redressed.) *Karen Shaker Collection.*

The largest *Kewpie* doll of all is the 27-inch (69cm) Strombecker from the early 1970s. This all-original doll has a vinyl head and a plastic body. The only markings are "Cameo ©" on the head and back.

Strombecker with a jointed head, 13in (33cm). *Shirley Karaba Collection.*

In the seated position, the *Kewpie Bunny* measures 9in (23cm). The mask face is vinyl; the remainder of the doll is corduroy and plush with wired ears and is a one-piece construction. The cloth tag denotes that this is from Knickerbocker in 1972-1973.

Mask-face *Kewpie* girl, 14in (36cm). From 1972-1973 by Knickerbocker. The face is vinyl; the remainder of the one-piece doll is stuffed cloth. The legend "© KNICKERBOCKER" is molded into the face under the chin.

Two one-piece Knickerbocker dolls with a vinyl mask face. The one with the high hat is 13in (33cm); the other one has a music box inside and it is 15in (38cm). *Shirley Karaba Collection.*

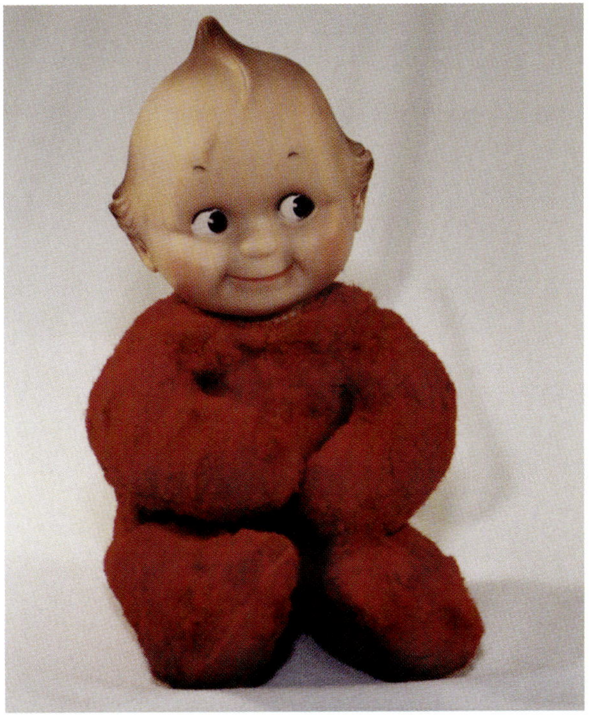

Doll with a vinyl head and plush body marked "Cameo," 12½in (32cm). However, it is likely a Knickerbocker doll, as the material matches other similar Knickerbocker *Kewpies. Shirley Karaba Collection.*

Right: *Ragsy Kewpie*, 10¾in (27cm). Probably by Amsco. *Shirley Karaba Collection.*

Amsco *Ragsy Kewpie,* 7½in (19cm). From mid-1970s made of vinyl with a jointed head. This is the original packaging. It is a plastic bag with a cardboard header with a hole punched in it for display on a retail rack. *Karen Shaker Collection.*

Right: Amsco No. 1206 *Kuddly Kewpie,* 8in (20cm). In the original package with a plastic front from 1974. The doll is fully-jointed.

Amsco No. 1208, 9½in (24cm). In the original package, 1974. Jointed head only.

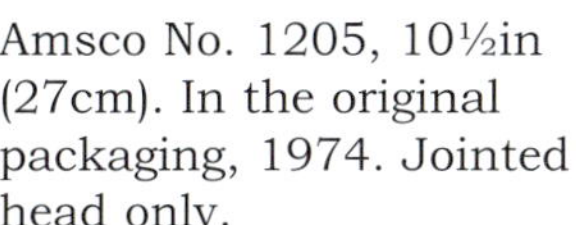

Amsco No. 1205, 10½in (27cm). In the original packaging, 1974. Jointed head only.

Amsco all-original *Kewpie*, $8\frac{1}{2}$in (22cm). Fully-jointed; from about 1973. The old-fashioned costume was a special to celebrate *Kewpie's* 60th Birthday. *Karen Shaker Collection.*

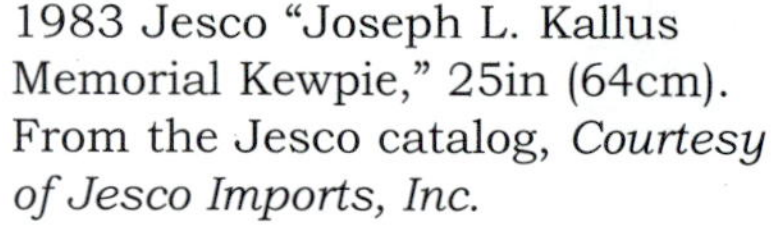

1983 Jesco "Joseph L. Kallus Memorial Kewpie," 25in (64cm). From the Jesco catalog, *Courtesy of Jesco Imports, Inc.*

"*Kewpie* Goes to School," 12in (31cm). Fully-jointed vinyl, #2105, 1983. *Shirley Karaba Collection.*

Fully-jointed "Bridesmaid" and "Best Man," 12in (31cm). From the Jesco *Kewpie* wedding party, 1980s. *Karen Shaker Collection.*

Jesco black *Kewpie,* 16in (41cm). *Karen Shaker Collection.*

Kewpie baby, 21in (53cm). Vinyl head and soft cloth body by Jesco. *Karen Shaker Collection.*

Right: Jesco Sailors, 12in (31cm). *Karen Shaker Collection.*

All-original *Kewpie*, 12in (31cm). From 1987. *Karen Shaker Collection.*

75th Anniversary Kewpie by Jesco in the 12-inch (31cm) size, 1988. *Karen Shaker Collection.*

Top right: *Kewpie* "Jester," 8in (20cm). Designed by Nancy Villaseñor-Cordaro for a Special Luncheon at the 1988 UFDC Convention in Anaheim, California. The fully-jointed vinyl doll was made in China.

Right: Spanish boy and girl in the 12-inch (31cm) size by Jesco. *Photograph Courtesy of Jesco Imports, Inc.*

Four styles of Jesco's *Kewpie,* 8in (20cm). *Photograph Courtesy of Jesco Imports Inc.*

Three styles of *Kewpie* girls, 8in (20cm). *Photograph Courtesy of Jesco Imports, Inc.*

Jesco *Christmas Kewpie*, 8in (20cm). Circa 1990. *Photograph Courtesy of Jesco Imports, Inc.*

Right: Clown, 16in (41cm). *Photograph Courtesy of Jesco Imports, Inc.*

Jesco *Kewpies,* 16in (41cm). Dressed in prints featuring dots, stripes and cars. *Photograph Courtesy of Jesco Imports, Inc.*

Three Jesco *Kewpies,* 16in (41cm). Made as Collectors' Specials for a television promotion on QVC. *Photograph Courtesy of Jesco Imports, Inc.*

Two Jesco *Kewpies,* 16in (41cm). Made as Collectors' Specials for a television promotion on QVC. *Photograph Courtesy of Jesco Imports, Inc.*

Three *Kewpies* in formal costumes, 16in (41cm). *Photograph Courtesy of Jesco Imports, Inc.*

Porcelain *Kewpie*,14in (36cm). This was a QVC Special. *Photograph Courtesy of Jesco Imports, Inc.*

Limited Edition Porcelain *Kewpie*, 25in (64cm). *Photograph Courtesy of Jesco Imports, Inc.*

Above: Rose Art *Kewpie,* 7½in (19cm). In the original packaging, 1993. *Karen Shaker Collection.*

Above: Another Rose Art vinyl, 7½in (19cm). Fully-jointed, 1993. *Shirley Karaba Collection.*

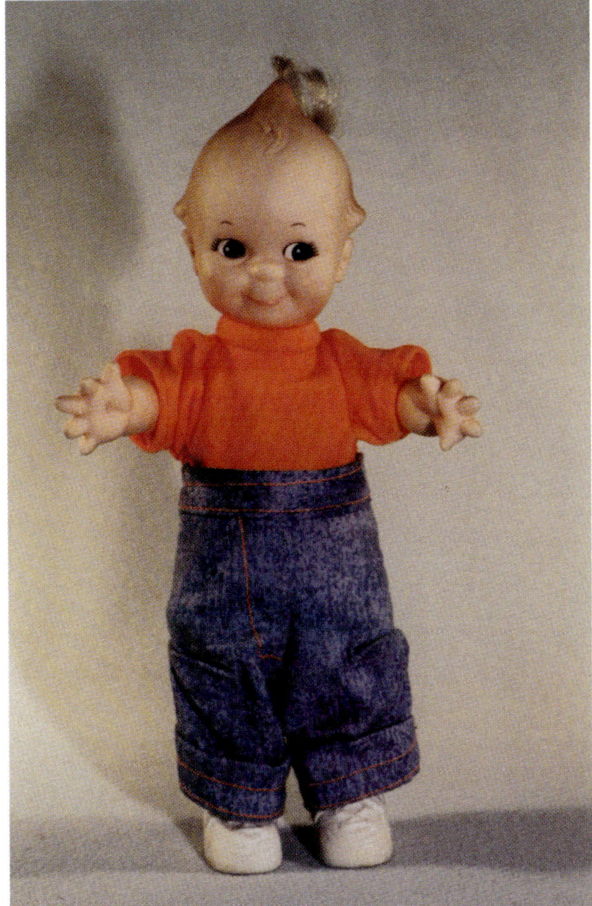

Fully-jointed vinyl *Kewpie*, 9in (23cm). A play doll from Rose Art, circa 1993. *Shirley Karaba Collection.*

Kewpie

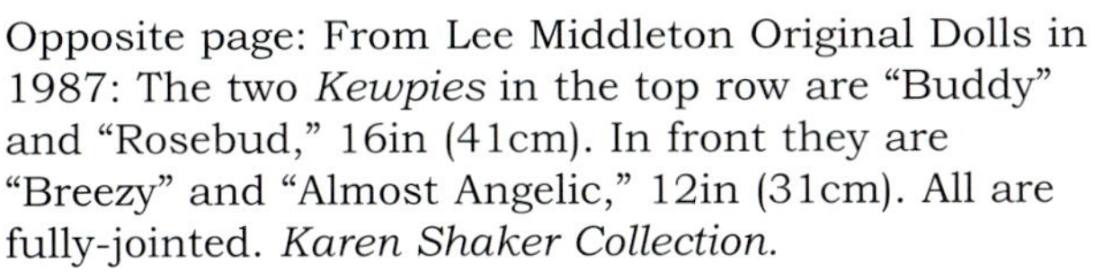

Opposite page: From Lee Middleton Original Dolls in 1987: The two *Kewpies* in the top row are "Buddy" and "Rosebud," 16in (41cm). In front they are "Breezy" and "Almost Angelic," 12in (31cm). All are fully-jointed. *Karen Shaker Collection.*

Rose Art *Kewpie* in baby form, 17in (43cm). Soft body and a vinyl head, 1993. *Karen Shaker Collection.*

Left: Two fully-jointed dolls, a special by Effanbee, made in China. The "Guardian Angel," 16in (41cm) and the "Millennium Baby," 8in (20cm). Limited to 2000 pieces. Designed by Margiann Flanagan.

Above: From the "*Kewpie* Romper Room" by Effanbee, marked 1999 for 2000 production. These are based on the designs that Effanbee used for *Kewpies* in the late 1940s. Made in China of "collector quality hard vinyl." The sizes are 8in (20cm), 12in (31cm) and 16in (41cm). *Karen Shaker Collection.*

Below: Production was limited to the year 2001 for "Snow White and Her Seven *Kewpies*," a very clever concept by Effanbee. These fully-jointed "collector quality hard vinyl" dolls were made in China. Snow White is 16in (41cm) tall; the Seven *Kewpies* are each 8in (20cm). The names of the seven are, going clock-wise from the top left: Twig, Nutmeg, Cork, Lucky, Thistle, Seedling, and Bucky (based on the names given in the Effanbee 2001 catalog). *Karen Shaker Collection.*

"*Kewpie* Romper Room," 16in (41cm). *Karen Shaker Collection.*

"*Kewpie* Halloween," 8in (20cm). By Effanbee, 2000. Made in China. *Karen Shaker Collection.*

"Holiday *Kewpie,*" 12in (31cm). By Effanbee, 2001. Made in China. *Karen Shaker Collection.*

Goldberger *Kewpie Baby*, 12in (31cm). Made in China, 2000. This doll has a cloth body. The white streak at the head is a glare caused by lights on the window box in which she is presented. *Karen Shaker Collection.*

Top: Goldberger "Mini Kewps," 4in (10cm). Made in China, 2000. These vinyl dolls probably have jointed heads and arms. From left to right: "Angel", "Bride", "Ballerina." *Karen Shaker Collection.*

Middle: Goldberger "Mini Kewps," 4in (10cm). Made in China, 2000. These vinyl dolls probably have jointed heads and arms. From left to right: "Bunny", "Birthday", "Cheerleader." *Karen Shaker Collection.*

Goldberger "Mini Kewp Cheerleader," 4in (10cm). *Karen Shaker Collection.*

Above: Goldberger *Kewpies* as storybook characters, 7½in (19cm). From left to right: "Angel", "Little Bo Peep", "Little Red Riding Hood", and "Alice in Wonderland." Made in China, 1999. *Karen Shaker Collection.*

Goldberger *Kewpie* as "Little Red Riding Hood," 7½in (19cm). *Karen Shaker Collection.*

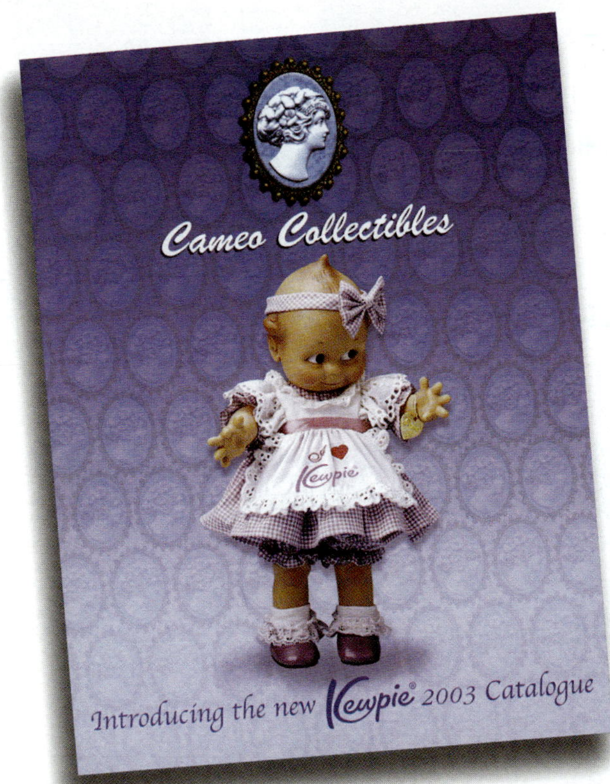

The 2003 Cameo Collectibles Catalogue, featuring 12-inch (31cm) "I Love Grandma," #V3061B. The name Cameo for this new company was chosen in honor of Joseph L. Kallus who founded the original Cameo company. *Courtesy of Joe Bartolotta.*

Scootles

Circa 1929+ **Cameo Doll Company**; distributed by others, including **Effanbee**	**Composition**
	Jointed arms, legs and head; painted eyes or sleep eyes; painted hair.
	8in (20cm)
	9½in (24cm)
	12½in (32cm)
	14in (36cm)
	15½in (39cm)
	21in (53cm)
Circa 1929+	**All-bisque**
	Made in Germany; Made in Japan (including "knock offs")
	Jointed only at arms:
	5-6in (13-15cm)
Circa 1930s	**Cloth**
	10in (25cm)
	19in (48cm)
	other sizes
	Vinyl
	Fully-jointed
1964-1970s	**Cameo Doll Co.**
	Sizes:
	9-11in (23-28cm)
	12in (31cm)
	14in (36cm)
	16in (41cm)
1984-1995	**Jesco Imports, Inc.**
	11in (28cm)
1997	**Lee Middleton Original Dolls, Inc.**
	"Commemorative Doll Postage Stamp Series"
	12in (31cm)

Fully-jointed composition *Scootles,* 12½in (32cm). Made by Cameo, circa 1940s. This doll is all-original, including the hang tag on the arm. *Rosemary Hanline Collection.*

Below: Fully-jointed composition versions of *Scootles*, 12½in (32cm) and 15½in (39cm). Produced in 1930s-1940s. *Shirley Karaba Collection.*

Black version of the fully-jointed composition *Scootles*, 12½in (32cm). Probably from the 1940s and distributed by Effanbee. Everything is original and perfect, including the painted eyes. *Shirley Karaba Collection.*

Fully-jointed vinyl *Scootles,* 9in (23cm) with the original box. Cameo, circa 1960s *Shirley Karaba Collection.*

Above: Black vinyl *Scootles,* 11in (28cm). Fully-jointed doll by Jesco, 1980s. Made in China. *Shirley Karaba Collection.*

Above right: Bisque black *Scootles,* 14in (36cm). Made by Jesco, a QVC Special. *Photograph Courtesy of Jesco Imports, Inc.*

Right: In 1997, the U.S. Postal Service printed a set of fifteen stamps featuring American-made dolls from antique examples to modern ones. Doll collectors felt that it was a huge mistake to feature *Scootles* instead of Rose O'Neill's *Kewpie*, one of the most famous dolls of all time. Nevertheless, this is better than no recognition for Rose O'Neill. This photograph shows an original composition *Scootles* as it appeared on the stamp with an all-vinyl 12-inch (31cm) version made by Lee Middleton Original Dolls, Inc., one of the "Commemorative Doll Postage Stamp Series." Copyright and registration information was given for the USPS, Rita Abraham and Jesco. *Photograph courtesy of Jesco Imports, Inc.*

Giggles

1946+ **Noma Electric (Effanbee)**	**Composition**
	Fully-jointed with painted eyes and hair.
	Hair has a loop molded into it for a ribbon.
	12in (31cm)

Giggles by Cameo, 12in (31cm). Distributed by Effanbee, late 1940s. Note her name that is on a *Kewpie* box with an applied label. This is #9613 and is fully-jointed composition with painted eyes. *Shirley Karaba Collection.*

Shirley Karaba's mint condition *Giggles* from the late 1940s.

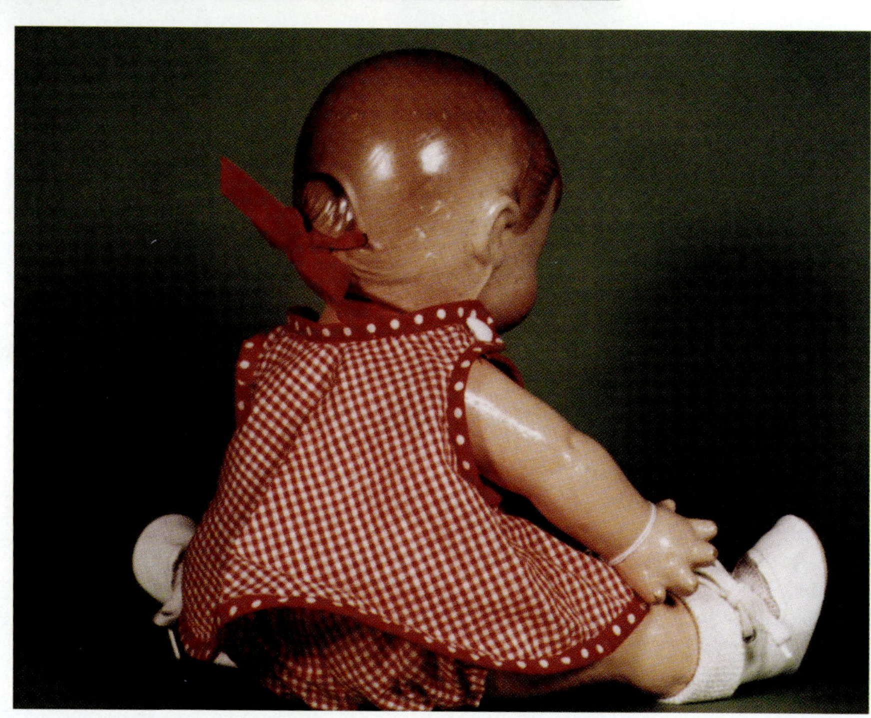

Above: Another all-original mint composition *Giggles,* 12in (31cm). From the 1940s. *Rosemary Hanline Collection.*

Right: Back view of Rosemary Hanline's *Giggles*, showing the molded loop in her hair for a ribbon.

Kewpie Gal

Made by Strombecker and Amsco with credit to Cameo from about 1969 to 1976; made by Jesco, Inc. in the 1980s.	**Vinyl** Fully-jointed with molded hair with slots for a hair ribbon. This is basically a *Kewpie* doll with molded "hair." The bodies were *Kewpie* bodies. 11in (28cm)

Fully-jointed vinyl *Kewpie Gal*, 11in (28cm). Circa early 1970s, possibly by Amsco and wearing an original costume. *Shirley Karaba Collection.*

Danbury Mint

Danbury Mint bisque dolls, 12in (31cm). Each *Kewpie* is fully-jointed with inset glass eyes. These dolls were made in China under very high production values and they sold for $89.00, which is reasonable considering their quality. "From *Kewpie* with Love" was the first one. All of these dolls are dated "1997," except for "*Kewpie* Bride and Groom," which are from 1998. *Karen Shaker Collection.*

On the left is the Danbury Mint's "Gift of Love" and on the right is "From *Kewpie* with Love."

On the left is "Bringing You Laughter" and on the right is "Gift from the Sea." Note *Kewpie's* accessories.

"Be Mine." Note the high-quality details, such as the shoes and sox.

Kewpie "Bride and Groom."

Chapter 4

Porcelain Kewpie Figurines in the Jesco Era

Manufactured *Kewpie* likenesses have come full circle. By the 1980s, genuine licensed products by various importers were once again made from porcelain bisque. These figurines were made in Asia with one notable exception. During recent times, *Kewpies* were also made of a modern material called cold-cast porcelain, a form of resin or plastic. Cold-cast porcelain permits a product to capture many fine details that would not be possible with fired porcelain or bisque. These modern pieces have been produced under license from Rita Abraham or Jesco. Many of these *Kewpies* are original designs and poses of Rose O'Neill's beloved creation.

The *Kewpies* from the company called Extra Special, Inc. are nicely finished. They were made in Korea in about 1985. One problem with the designs is that these *Kewpies* are involved in "romantic" themes, which does not seem quite appropriate for the childlike character of *Kewpies.* In contrast, the Franklin Mint porcelain *Kewpies* produced in the early 1990s are all involved in activities befitting their perceived and relative ages. These twelve models were crafted in Thailand, another Asian country that exported high-quality porcelain at the time.

Most of the bisque *Kewpie* figurines made by Enesco in the early 1990s were produced in Indonesia. Enesco has always been known for its high-quality porcelain (or bisque) production. Enesco has produced many different series of licensed characters such as the *Lucy & Me Teddy Bears*, and there are usually a large number of designs for each series.

The Danbury Mint crafts some of the very best porcelain, or bisque, dolls and figurines on the current market. The company obtained a *Kewpie* license in 1994 though production seems to begin at the end of the 1990s. Collectors appreciate the accurate and careful details found in this company's accessories. For example, shoes are authentic if they are for reproduction dolls; wigs and eyes are made in scale and are appropriate. Many doll companies no longer try to achieve correctness in these details of finishing, although cost considerations are negligible. The Danbury Mint figurines, whether of traditional porcelain or modern resins, have more details and originality of design than those of most contemporary firms producing comparable products.

The German Doll Company, founded by Susan Bickert and Roland Schlegel, has been producing *Kewpie* figurines since 1999. These figurines are of special interest as they were created from the original molds of 1913 to 1918 from the Hermann Voigt and Hertwig factories of Germany. The mold inventory was purchased from individuals in Germany who had maintained them in perfect condition. Several different *Kewpie* designs, including many rare models, were made in Germany in recent years from the original molds. Now some *Kewpie* designs are produced in China. The latest *Kewpies* from China have the best finishing and painting of any porcelain *Kewpie* figurines since before World War I.

Two figurines by Extra Special, 3½in (9cm). From 1985. Made in Korea. *Bette Ann Axe Collection.*

Makers of *Kewpie* figurines since 1983:

Extra Special, Inc.
1985-1987 (?)

The Franklin Mint
1990-1991

Enesco Imports Corp.
1992-1997

The Danbury Mint
1994+

The German Doll Company
1999+

Bride And Groom called "Forever Yours," 4in (10cm). By Extra Special, 1985. *Karen Shaker Collection.*

"Parade of Love" music box, 6in (15cm). By Extra Special, 1985. *Karen Shaker Collection.*

"Sweet Serenade," 4in (10cm). By Extra Special, Item No. 5160, 1985. Made in Korea.

The twelve bisque figurines by The Franklin Mint in 1991. They came with a glass case to display them in with the logo *"KEWPIE"* on it. The tallest one is 4½in (12cm). Printed on the bottom are copyright and trademark information and "© 1990 FM." Crafted in Thailand.

Close-up of Franklin Mint bisque figurine of 1991.

Enesco bisque figurines made in Indonesia. *Kewpie* with a dog, 4¼in (11cm) marked, "1991." The *Kewpidoodle Dog* wearing reindeer horns is from 1994.

Enesco Kewp with a goose, 4¼in (11cm). Copyright 1991. Crafted in Indonesia. *Shirley Karaba Collection.*

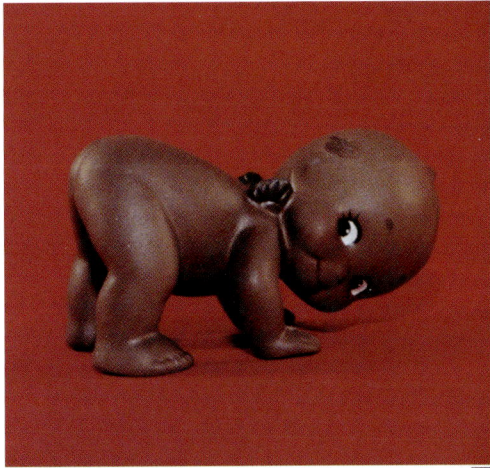

Enesco's black *Kewpie,* 1¼in (3cm). Made in Taiwan in 1992.

Two Enesco figurines made in Indonesia. The taller one is from 1992; the shorter one from 1993. Both are with their original boxes. *Shirley Karaba Collection.*

Left: Enesco figurines, 3¾in (10cm) and 4¼in (11cm). Copyrighted in 1993 and made in Indonesia. *Bette Ann Axe Collection.*

Enesco Christmas tree ornaments from 1992-1994, averaging about 3½in (9cm) long. Made in Indonesia. All are bisque except for a *Kewpie* riding a scooter, which is of plastic. Note that all are colored in pale and pastel shades. *Karen Shaker Collection.*

This set by Enesco from 1994 is one of the most unique Christmas Nativity groupings ever made. "Baby Jesus" lies in a teacup; "Joseph" carries a spoon for a staff; the "Little Drummer Boy" bangs on a tea strainer. Made in Indonesia. The tallest figure is 4¼in (11cm). *Karen Shaker Collection.*

Two Halloween figurines by Enesco, 1995. *Photographs Courtesy of Jesco Imports, Inc.*

Two Christmas figurines by Enesco, 1995. *Photographs Courtesy of Jesco Imports, Inc.*

The twelve Danbury Mint bisque Christmas ornaments from 2000. They are painted in brighter colors than the Enesco ornaments. Made in China. Average size is about 3½in (9cm). *Karen Shaker Collection.*

There are eight Danbury Mint figurines called the "*Kewpie* Trio Sculptures." They were made of resin in China in 1998, 1999 and 2000. They measure about 6-8in (15-20cm) tall. *Karen Shaker Collection.*

"Ring Around the May Pole," 2000.

"He Loves Me, He loves Me Not," 1999.

"Colorful Trio," 2000.

"The Spirit of *Kewpies*," 1999.

"Angelic *Kewpie*," 1998.

"Make a Wish," 2000.

"On the Open Seas," 2000.

"Lessons to Live By," 2000.

Opposite page: *Kewpie* Calendar with 3-3½in (8-9cm) figures. Licensed to the Danbury Mint by Jesco in 2001. Each *Kewpie* figurine was made in China of resin. As of this writing (early 2003), monthly figurines are still being mailed to subscribers. *Photograph Courtesy of Jesco Imports, Inc*

APRIL
JANUARY
I LOVE YOU
FEBRUARY
MARCH
S M T W T F S
Kewpie 1 2 3 4 5 6
8 9 10 11 12 13
15 16 17 18 19 20
21 22 23 24 25 26 27
28 29 30 Kewpie Kewpie Kewpie Kewpie
Kewpie Kewpie Kewpie Kewpie Kewpie Kewpie Kewpie
MAY
JUNE
JULY
AUGUST
E=MC2
SEPTEMBER
OCTOBER
NOVEMBER
DECEMBER

Bisque "*Kewpie* Thinker" as a 2000 Christmas tree ornament, 3in (8cm). Made by The German Doll Company under license to Jesco with original molds. *Shirley Karaba Collection.*

"German Soldier *Kewpie*," 4in (10cm). Made of bisque by The German Doll Company from the original molds. *Shirley Karaba Collection.*

Kewpie riding a goat and riding an elephant, 4½in (12cm). Made in Germany by The German Doll Company. They are from the original molds. These *Kewpies* riding animals were originally produced in Germany by the Hermann Voigt Porcelain Factory before World War I. *Courtesy of Susan Bickert/The German Doll Company.*

Kewpie doll with jointed arms, 8½in (22cm). Made from the original mold by The German Doll Company. This was a souvenir for a UFDC Luncheon at the 2002 National Convention in Denver, Colorado. *Shirley Karaba Collection.*

Above: *Kewpies* riding animals, 4½in (12cm). Produced by The German Doll Company, from original molds. *Susan Bickert/German Doll Company samples.*

Kewpie riding a Dachshund, 4½in (12cm). By The German Doll Company, circa 2000, made in Germany from the original Hermann Voigt mold. *Karen Shaker Collection.*

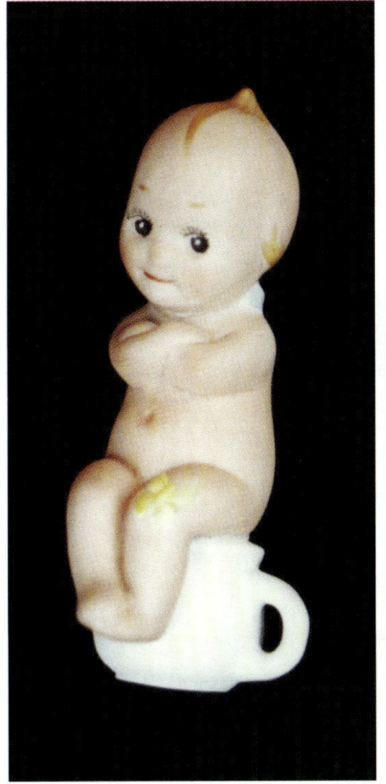

Kewpie sitting on a pot, 3in (8cm). Made in Germany by The German Doll Company from the original mold. *Susan Bickert/German Doll Company samples.*

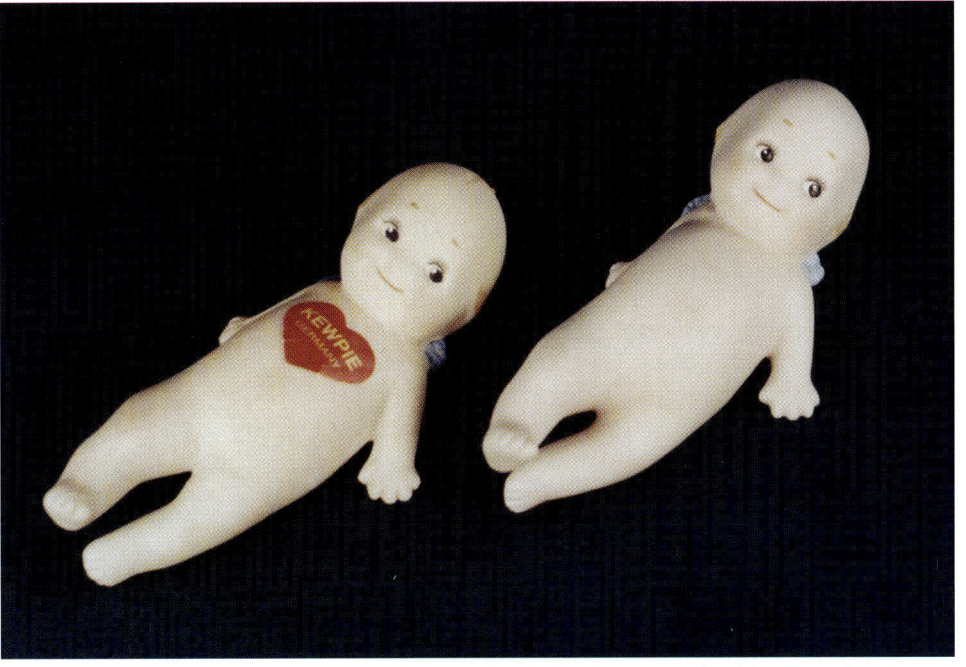

Above: *Kewpies* by The German Doll Company, 4in (10cm). Made from the original molds. The one on the left with a heart sticker on its chest was made in Germany; the one on the right was made in China. *Susan Bickert/German Doll Company samples.*

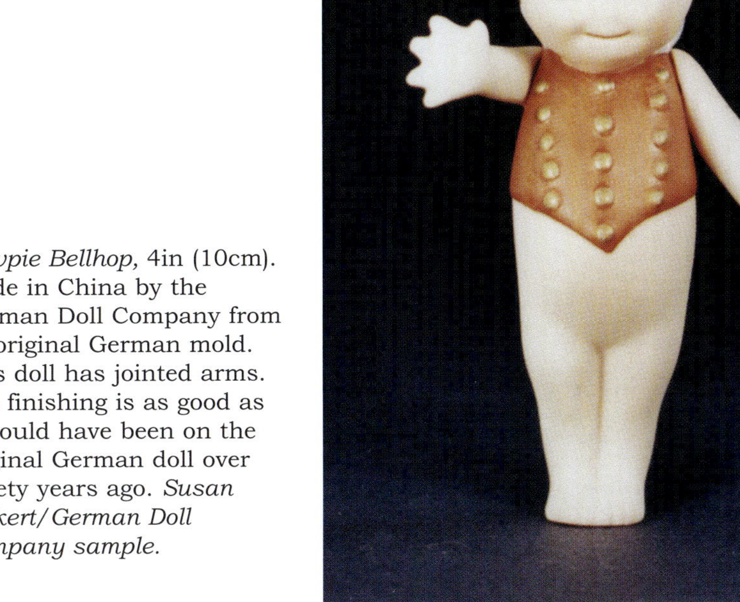

Kewpie Bellhop, 4in (10cm). Made in China by the German Doll Company from an original German mold. This doll has jointed arms. The finishing is as good as it would have been on the original German doll over ninety years ago. *Susan Bickert/German Doll Company sample.*

Conclusion

As of this writing (2003) it is 129 years since Rose O'Neill's birth and 94 years after she first published pictures of her *Kewpies* in *The Ladies' Home Journal.* Since 1909, *Kewpies* have appeared in many different media. There have also been several kinds of unauthorized or "knock-off" *Kewpie* forms. Collectors are just as interested in *Kewpie*® as they ever were because *Kewpie* has always retained his, or her, charm. The *Kewpie* likeness has been the property of four different entities: Geo. Borgfeldt & Co., Rose O'Neill, Joseph L. Kallus/Rita Abraham, and Jesco Imports, Inc. They have protected *Kewpie* well.

Other than the examples of *Kewpie* forms seen in this book, Jesco has also licensed the *Kewpie* image to the McCall Pattern Company for patterns featuring *Kewpie*; to Mental Inc., a company that makes active wear; to Nick & Nora, a manufacturer of upscale sleepwear for adults; Current, Inc. for personal bank checks; Collegeville/Imagineering, LP for costumes and masks; Gimbles of Maine for USPS *Scootles* stamp thimble; and The March Company for metal pins of the *Scootles* stamp. As we have seen, more doll and toy companies than ever before are manufacturing collectibles for adults that feature *Kewpies.*

Kewpie, the cutest little imp that ever was, will no doubt be created in new images for many generations to come. *Kewpie*® will assure that the name Rose O'Neill is well known forever.

Index

About the Author

Hobby House Press has published many books for collectors by John Axe since his first one in 1977. He is a widely recognized and respected authority in the doll and toy-collecting hobby. He is the author of many well-received books in this field, including *The Encyclopedia of Celebrity Dolls*, which is now considered a classic research volume. Among others are *The Magic of Merrythought* (a revised edition was published in England) and *Effanbee: A Collector's Encyclopedia*, both of which deal with the production of a single toy company. His hundreds of articles about doll and teddy bear collecting have appeared in several publications, including *Teddy Bear and Friends, Paper Doll Review, Doll Reader, Contemporary Doll Collector* and *Doll News*, the journal of UFDC (the United Federation of Doll Clubs, Inc.). He was also editor of *Doll News* for six years, as well as editor of three UFDC annual Souvenir Journals. He has also edited many books by other authors who wrote about collectibles and has contributed to several other research books, the most recent being *The Barrymores*, published by the University Press of Kentucky. His latest research books from Hobby House Press are about collecting girls' and boys' series books, a subject about which he also publishes many articles and booklets.

John Axe has been an active member of UFDC for many years and has been appointed to several positions in the national organization, including Chairman of the Modern Competitive Exhibit and Chairman of Judges. He served as president of three UFDC clubs—The Pittsburgh Doll Club, Les Rubans Aubergine and After Dark Doll Study Club of Ohio.

Mr. Axe is also an artist who has won prizes for his paper doll art of vintage characters and costumes. He has done paper doll souvenirs and souvenir books for numerous paper doll conventions. Hobby House Press has also published eight of his paper doll books. John has designed a number of teddy bears and other animals that were produced by Merrythought Limited, England's oldest continuing toy company.

John Axe holds a degree in Spanish Studies from the University of Valladolid in Spain, an AB and MA from Youngstown State University in Ohio and was a Ph.D. Candidate at The University of Akron. He taught Spanish and History at Penn State University and Youngstown State University for many years. Now he concentrates on his hobbies.

Other Books by John Axe

Collectible Boy Dolls
Collectible Dolls in National Costume
The Collectible Dionne Quintuplets
Collectible Black Dolls
Collectible Patsy Dolls and Patsy-Types
Collectible Sonja Henie
Tammy and Dolls You Love to Dress
The Encyclopedia of Celebrity Dolls
Effanbee: A Collector's Encyclopedia
Celebrity Doll Price Guide and Annual (with A. Glenn Mandeville)
The Magic of Merrythought
Kewpies: Dolls & Art of Rose O'Neill and Joseph L. Kallus
The Best of John Axe
Tammy and Her Family of Dolls
The Secret of Collecting Girls' Series Books
All About Collecting Girls' Series Books
All About Collecting Boys' Series Books

Paper Doll Books by John Axe

Romantic Heroes of Fiction
Royal Children: Queen Victoria to Queen Elizabeth II
Figure Skating Champions
Country Music Singers
Effanbee's Wee Patsy Paper Dolls and Playhouse
Effanbee's Wee Patsy Paper Dolls and Playhouse—Wee Edition
Effanbee's Patsyette
Effanbee's Candy Kid & Honey